DEVELOP YOUR LATENT PARANORMAL POWERS

An Eleven Lesson Course

DragonStar

&

Sir William Walker Atkinson

Inner Light Publications
New Brunswick, NJ 08903

DEVELOP YOUR LATENT PARANORMAL POWERS

by Dragonstar and Sir William Walker Atkinson

Cover Art by Tim Swartz

Editorial consultant, Carol Ann Rodriguez

Timothy Green Beckley, Publisher

ISBN: 1-892062-45-3

Request a free catalog from Inner Light Publications
Box 753, New Brunswick, NJ 08903
A free subscription to the Conspiracy Journal is
available on the net at
www.conspiracyjournal.com
Credit card orders 732 602-3407

Develop Your Latent Paranormal Powers

DRAGONSTAR

Your Journey Has Begun

Much has been written about the world of psychic phenomena and the powers of the human mind and its wide reaching potential. Even our astronauts have sent telepathic waves from the surface of the moon to see if someone on earth could read their minds.

ESP is sort of "old hat." We've all seen movies like **Ghostbusters** and **Mothman Prophecies** and fully realize and that there is an entire invisible universe that surrounds and permeates us. These energies extend beyond what we know as the material world and we can tap into these mystic forces to create and maintain our desires and goals.

Years ago, my co-author Sir William Walker Atkinson discovered the many possibilities of paranormal powers. He was well ahead of his time as this 11 lesson study course plainly shows. But I, Dragonstar the living master of a clan of magicians whose roots extend back to the ancient land of Atlantis will now reveal secrets of our paranormal world to further promote the possibilities of the supernormal, psychic abilities, and the supernatural.

These amazing powers are available to all who are willing to throw off the shackles of our everyday lives and lift the veil that hides the unlimited potentials that the universe has waiting for us. Before you start, take ten minutes to meditate on the cover of this book. Ask yourself what it is you want out of life and what kinds of paranormal powers that you want to develop and use. Now, as you read these words, you are already being infused with the white light of unlimited universal energy.

You are now ready to begin your journey to enlightenment and spiritual growth. With this growth come great powers and abilities that seem almost too fantastic to believe. Abilities such as contacting the ascended masters, mind reading, telekinesis, astral journeys to other worlds, time travel and much more.

Read carefully the contents of the amazing book — for once you begin your quest, you cannot go back, you will not want to go back. Your old life will seem like a hazy dream, without focus or purpose. While your new life will be filled with incredible adventures and a new, more vivid way of looking at the world around you.

Contacting The Ascended Masters

One of the first things that you should do on your journey to enlightenment is to learn how to contact the Ascended Masters. These are highly advanced spiritual beings who are waiting to act as guides to those who are ready to grow and develop as enlightened beings of spiritual energy.

The Ascended Masters are available to everyone who asks for their help. You do not need to be an experienced channel or be a person who is well versed in spiritual matters for them to help you or teach you. They will always do their best to help you meet your goals for spiritual advancement and to help you with any problems that you have in your life in any way that they can.

Anyone can learn to channel. Channeling is a matter of opening to the love, energy, and conscious connection of a higher dimensional being. It is a tool that can be used in many ways. It is not only for relaying information.

When you meditate and feel the energy and love of your

higher self or a guide, you are channeling. You are channeling their energy, even if you do not receive a conscious word or thought from them. Most people channel and receive guidance and information from their higher self or a guide and are not aware that they are channeling.

Many people receive information or guidance in the dream state or through sudden inspirational thoughts. Some people channel while they are working on art, music or other creative expressions. Most people experience this form of channeling in their everyday lives. People have always been able to channel. It is not a new or recent phenomenon. The Bible and other Holy books are full of channeled material and channeling experiences.

All people are spiritual beings who are a part of a very advanced higher self. Each person is very connected to their higher self even if it is not a very conscious connection. Anyone can learn to channel and open that connection, not only to their higher self, but to all higher dimensional beings and to all that is.

There is nothing to fear when you channel. If it is your intention to open to your higher self and work only with them, then only your higher self will be there with you while you are reaching out to them. The higher self connection is a very powerful one. It is very helpful to establish a good higher self connection before channeling other beings.

It is a good idea to always ask your higher self to help you when you channel others. They can help you to establish a channeling connection with any higher dimensional guide or teacher that you wish to work with. So there is no need to fear that you will get into contact with a being that you do not wish to talk to.

Your higher self can make sure you are connected with the being you want to work with. You do have free will and can talk to anyone that you want, but we strongly suggest that you always work through your higher self and only with your own guides or very advanced universal teachers.

If you are channeling a guide with the help of your higher self it is easier to make the connection with that guide. Working through your higher self also helps you to interpret the information given by a guide in a clearer way. Your higher self knows you better than anyone else. If you are getting the information from a guide or universal teacher through your higher self, they can more easily help put the information into words and ideas that you can more readily understand and accept.

Your intentions and requests have everything to do with what happens when you channel. It is best to have in mind whom you want to work with and what kind of work that you wish to do before you start to channel. Each time before you start to channel or meditate, invite in whom you wish to work with and state what you want to accomplish in that session.

Learning to be a channel for universal or spiritual information to share with others may not be what everyone would like to do. But each person can learn to channel the love and energy of their higher self and other higher dimensional beings. Each person can establish a very conscious connection with their higher self, guides and Ascended Masters, for their own information and spiritual growth and help in their everyday lives.

There are many ways that you can learn to channel for information. One of the easiest is to simply sit quietly and ask that your higher self or a guide connect with you consciously and energetically. Once the connection is made, try to be as open as you can be to the thoughts and words that they will send you. You can just be aware of the thoughts and words, or you can repeat the information that you are getting out loud. If you are comfortable with it you can ask to connect with them in a more complete way and have them speak through you.

When you have established a good conscious connection with your higher self or guide and are comfortable channeling them, you can ask to work with a universal teacher, such as an Ascended Master or Archangel. The process is the same whether you are channeling your own higher self or any other higher dimensional being. It is no harder to channel an Ascended Master or an Archangel than it is to channel your higher self.

They will always come to you in a way that you are ready for and capable of.

As you learn, grow, and develop your channeling abilities they can come to you in more and more expanded ways, but right from the start you can work with their energy and benefit from their love and guidance. The more that you accept yourself as the spiritual being, the easier it will be to open to the love and wisdom that is available to you. That frame of mind prepares you to work with your higher self, guides, and all universal teachers in a more expanded way.

The Art Of Psychic Mind Reading

This hidden power is available to those who recognize and accept that there is a higher realm of knowing and communication beyond their own physical bodies. The universe is full of this unlimited energy that can be tapped by almost anyone who will make the effort to focus and tune themselves to its subtle vibrations. These vibrations are not just for the so called 'gifted' persons, but for everyone who makes the effort to learn its secrets.

Most all psychic people are that because they recognized

the signs of this energy and focused their attention on its workings which is the very thing that is required in order to develop it. If they hadn't focused their attention on it, then they wouldn't be what they are.

To begin tuning into this force you need to learn about focusing. Focusing on even the smallest instance of psychic phenomena that happens to your self and to people around you. Play the event around in your mind continually, to get familiar with the sense of the action and presence of the energy involved. This will give you a perception of how involved and integrated is the underlying hidden power that caused the event to take place.

One of the most important things to understand is that every living thing, plants, animals, people, has consciousness and is connected to everything else in the universe. People, animals and plants are all connected to the hidden energy of universal consciousness that permeates the entire universe and 'wires' all of us together.

Understanding and accepting this simple concept is the most important requirement to developing one's own latent ability. The next important requirement, is that the person must have both a desire and willingness to develop and tune themselves so they can also connect with the universal spirit.

ESP — Extrasensory perception is the term used to describe a means of getting information from other than the five senses that everyone uses as their primary means. The five senses are seeing, feeling, smelling, tasting, and hearing. These are considered to be our 'normal' senses and any sense or gathering of information is said to be extra, or out of the ordinary.

When a person develops their ESP, they have increased their mind power by a quantum leap above other people. It enables them to send and receive information almost at will to influence things that are important to them.

Mind reading, clairvoyance, precognition are all perceived through mental telepathy. Mental telepathy makes possible the "knowing" about past future or current events that is not supposed to be part of our knowledge. When someone demonstrates an ability to send and receive information that is not part of their five ordinary senses, it is placed in the realm of "extra" almost as though it was bizarre or abnormal and not part of the human psyche or sense abilities. However, telepathic ability is available to all those willing to practice and learn how to increase this talent that is given to everyone at birth.

This is how clairvoyants, psychics and mediums know secret and private information about another person's life and are able to advise them. Some of them discovered that they had the ability at a young age and some not until later in their life. But they all have one thing in common. They made a decision not to ignore it, but rather to improve and cultivate it through patience, practice and effort. Many people can now benefit from their diligence and persistence in their own self development.

To become a psychic mind reader you must learn to switch your mindset from yourself and onto another person as the center point. Your focus is centered on the inner workings of that person as it relates to the world they live in. For this you need to go within to engage that part of yourself that communicates with the universal mind where all knowledge resides.

Just like learning any other skill you need to practice. Nothing comes to anyone without practice and reading another person is no different. Remember, you already have the ability, you only need to tune it and refine it. Mind set is important. The more serious you are about it, the faster you will develop your ability to give readings. If you are dedicated to learn, you will. Just remember, Rome was not built in a day, so be patient. Becoming a psychic mind reader requires patience and practice.

Meditation puts you on the fast track to developing your own potential. It helps you get in that deep inner part of yourself where you get help from outside — from the universal mind. If you don't meditate, you can still learn, but it takes a bit longer. Profound and meaningful information is more readily available for a person that meditates.

As each person goes through life, the events of that life are recorded. Every thought, words spoken, actions taken and not, are recorded with the universal mind. Some psychic readers refer to this as the Akashic Records, but its easier to visualize it as a video recording. This is information that you as a psychic reader can access.

The information comes through 5 sources:

1. *Feelings* -feelings that something is so, feelings of what a person is feeling inside, feelings about what a person fears, what is going on in their life, feelings about what is going on in regard to their personal relationships, etc.

2. *Pictures* - Visual pictures will come to the psychic reader, some are directly interpreted and others ate indirectly related. That is some pictures are symbols for another meaning. For example: in giving a reading, a woman client is visualized fishing off a bridge. Does it mean that the client is really going to go fishing or is she looking for a man? The answer lies in developing a 'feel' of how to interpret these symbols. And in this case, it turned out that the client was looking for a man.

3. *Hearing* - The psychic mind reader hears words in the form of mind talk. As though the psychic reader was talking to herself. Sometimes it seems like words are being imagined by you, the mind reader.

4. ***Knowing*** - One of the most profound ways that a psychic reader gets information is through 'knowing.' Suddenly, information appears. And as if by magic, the reader knows something that she didn't know a moment earlier.

5. ***Smelling and tasting*** - The psychic reader gets a sense (feels) of smelling or tasting.

Sometimes you will only get a single word or picture about a person which doesn't provide a clear meaning. You must then go back and ask that symbol to give you more information.

More information usually comes through one of the other sources. For example, the picture of the woman fishing on the bridge didn't give an explanation beyond the image itself When the reader went back for more information, a feeling came to her that the woman was really actively looking for a man to be in her life. The psychic mind reader goes back to the source as many times as necessary to get a coherent message for her client.

Spiritual growth is the by-product of psychic development. As you expand you own awareness of the universe through the experiences you get from these practices, you become more balanced and discerning. You will see the world and people from a different perspective. You'll see things as a whole rather than from their individual parts. And you will have a greater empathy because you'll understand what is going on in many people, even if they don't see it themselves.

Every day of our lives we engage in the paranormal practice of communicating with a higher realm of consciousness and we are not even aware of it. Following is a list of things that everyone has experienced at least once. Look them over and remember similar such psychic events that happened to you. Once you have become aware of them, practice them and more will occur. Through a higher awareness you can make the paranormal become the normal for you.

Here are a few types of events you should be looking for:

1. **Coincidences** - Pay attention to coincidences that amaze you, including those that don't. All coincidences have a meaning, especially if they seem to further your psychic or spiritual path. Record all of them.

2. **Hunches** - See what happens with your hunches. Take the effort to see if they play out as they came to you.

3. **Urges** - Follow up on urges. If you followed the urge, what happened? Did your inner urge match reality?

4. **The little inner voice** - Listen to it. Deep within it gives you an awareness and knowledge about yourself or someone else. About the present, past or future. We don't always hear it, because our conscious minds are preoccupied with ourselves. The subtlety of this voice sometimes makes us think that our mind is talking to itself Record these occasions to enhance your ability.

5. **Predictions** - If you are going to see someone that you've never met, try to picture in your mind what this person looks like. Practice advance awareness, by always trying to predict things in advance of seeing or experiencing them. This is a good method for getting immediate feedback.

Your Paranormal Wishing Device

If you have ever wanted a particular wish or desire to come true, but had trouble focusing your energies on this desire, here is a very simple, but amazingly powerful device that will help you focus your thoughts like a laser beam of energy.

First you need to write down just what it is you want. Do you need more money? Do you want a new and better job? Are you interested in someone and want them to be interested in you? Whatever it is you want, write it down. Keep your request short and to the point. "I will have more money!" "I will get a new and better job!" "I will attract the attention of the one I love." Don't write it down as a wish, make a power statement: "I will get my desire!"

Now take a regular sheet of white paper and roll it into a cone. Make sure the small end is left open to about an inch in diameter. You will need to see through this opening, so leave some room. Tape it together so it retains its shape.

Next you need to shape your energy into a compact ball of power. You cup your hands as if holding something between them, and then visualize yourself as a conduit of universal energy, and just let it flow out through your hands and into a ball between them. Imagine this ball of energy as white-hot and bursting with the paranormal energy that is needed to make your wish come true. You can tell if you are successful by paying attention to your hands. They will get hot and your hand will have little twitches every now and then.

When you have built the energy up to as high as you think you need, take your power cone and paper with your wish written on it — point the small end of the cone at your wish and visualize your ball of power entering the large end and being concentrated into a shaft of laser light. Read each word you have written down

XI

through the small end of the cone. Imagine the laser energy burning each word with its paranormal powers.

It is important that you keep your mind focused on the task at hand. You have accumulated a vast amount of power for your goal. Don't waste it on stray thoughts. Keep your one wish in mind at all times.

Continue to illuminate each word of your wish until you have run out of power. At that point, stop for the day. You can try again in 24 hours. Allow enough time for your batteries to recharge. This is a very powerful technique, so don't be fooled by how simple it seems. Because of this, make sure that your wish is something you really want. As the old saying goes: "Be careful what you wish for, because it just may come true."

You can also use this technique to influence the thoughts of others. Practice with a friend. Write one word down and build your energy ball. Using your cone of power, try and project your word to the mind of your friend. Imagine the laser light burning the word into energy and transmitting it across the distance to your friend. You'll be amazed how easy this works.

After awhile, you can learn to influence the thoughts of others by using your paranormal powers. The next time you are at a party or in the mall, practice this technique on someone who is seated nearby. As before, visualize your energy ball and with your mind, turn it into a shaft of powerful laser light. Take five deep breaths and quickly exhale them, don't hold them in. Choose someone who is nearby and has their back towards you.

Concentrate your laser beam onto the back of the head of your test subject. Don't stare, just keep your attention focused on this person. See the white beam of light leaving your body and entering the head of your test subject. You will soon see that this person will start to fidget and look around. Soon they will turn and look right in your direction. Success! You are on your way to developing your paranormal abilities to influence the thoughts of others.

Continue to practice this technique with your friends. (Don't tell them what you are doing however, as this will set up a psychic block that will be hard to break through.) Now, instead of just sending a laser beam, send a thought or command in this energy to the mind of your practice subject. Tell them to scratch their head, or get up to get a drink.

Use this ability wisely, don't abuse your power. The universe has a way of preventing people from taking unfair advantage of others, so don't waste your powers to harm, be sensitive to the thoughts and needs of others.

This paranormal potential manifests itself in many ways. Sometimes when we have to make decisions or take some form of action we know exactly what to do, but at other times and on similar circumstances we are not so sure of what action to take. People who always seem to be in the right place at the right time, and for whom good things happen with uncanny frequency, are not just plain lucky — they have an intuitive sense of choosing, deciding and how to act to a given situation. Intuitive revelations steer the course for man to discover and invent and creative talents to originate.

Developing your paranormal powers can be accomplished if you know when you are psychically active. You can then use this knowledge to react to current events and know what action to take immediately, what to delay to a better cyclical period. You will intuitively know what to do or not do when you know what days are likely to produce failure and what days are likely to produce success.

Our lives were meant to be lived and enjoyed to their fullest. But usually we become so caught up in the everyday trivialities of day-to-day living that we lose sight of what is really important. Most of us go about our daily lives in a sort of stupor. We live like robots that have been programmed to perform the same functions day after day wit no deviation from the program. We are asleep at the wheel with no desire to awaken and take control.

This is no way to live. Every day should be a new and different experience and we should greet it with the same excitement and expectations as a child greets Christmas morning or a trip to their favorite amusement park. We must shake ourselves awake and look about at the wonderful universe that we helped create and acknowledge the important role we play.

Our amazing paranormal powers should be considered a gift from The Creator. Because of this, we should always use these abilities for the betterment of ourselves and others.

The misuse of your paranormal powers can create situations that are not planned or desired. Mystics throughout the ages have warned that if you use your abilities to try and control or harm others, you will suffer the ill-effects of your misdeeds. That is why you should always use your talents in the spirit of love and kindness.

To insure the proper frame of mind when attempting to use your paranormal powers — start each day with this little mental exercise that will fill you with the proper energies.

Sit in a quiet place and close your eyes. Visualize a beam of bright, pure white light coming down from heaven and hitting the top of your head. This is the light of ultimate creation and love. Visualize this beam of cleansing light spreading throughout your entire body. Feel it enter the top of your head and flow down through the energy pathways of your body. You are now charged with the universal spirit and ready to go.

So come along and allow my fellow practitioner and co-writer to instruct you in the various ways to expand your awareness and metaphysical knowledge. I am sure that you will be as impressed as I was with what Sir William Walker Atkinson has to say and teach you. Set the foundation now that will assure you a comfortable secure tomorrow. Follow your heart and rekindle the flame which will lead you to successes beyond your dreams.

Practical Psychomancy

Sir William Walter Atkinson

Table Of Contents

Lesson I.
The Nature of Psychomancy

THE term "Psychomancy (pronounced, "sy-ko-man-see"), is derived from two Greek words, the first "psycho," meaning "the soul; the mind; the understanding" (and generally used to indicate "psychic" or unusual powers of the soul or mind); the second word, "mancy" meaning "to divine; to foresee, or foreknow; to detect secret things," — and in occult parlance, "to sense," or to receive impressions by the Astral Senses." So the word, as we use it, may be said to mean "Psychic Sensing," and in this work will be so used. The word "Psychomancer" means "one practicing Psychomancy;" and the word "Psychomantic" means "relating to Psychomancy."

The word "Clairvoyance" is frequently used by people to designate some of the phases of Psychomancy, but strictly speaking this term is incorrect when used in this sense, the true occult meaning of the word "Clairvoyance," being "transcendental vision, or the perception of beings on another plane, of existence—the seeing of disembodied souls, elementals, etc." And so, in this work, we shall consider the true phenomena of Clairvoyance, as distinct from that of Psychomancy.

In this work, we shall regard as the true phenomena of Psychomancy, all the various phenomena known as Psychometry; Crystal Gazing; Perceiving Distant Scenes; a perception of Past Events, and Indication of Future Events; either in the full waking state; the state of reverie; or the state of dreams.

And, so this work will examine, consider, and explain, the various phases of phenomena above indicated—in short, the phenomena of **"sensing" objects by means of Astral Senses**, omitting the phenomena of Clairvoyance, or seeing disembodied souls, etc., which we regard as belonging to a different phase of the general subject, and which require special consideration and examination.

The majority of works upon these lines begin by an elaborate attempt to "prove" the reality of the phenomena in question. But we shall not fall into this error, for such we regard it. The time for the necessity of such proof is past. The records of the Societies for Psychical Research are full of proofs, and evidence, which are as full, complete and strong as ever required by any court to hang or clear a man. And the book shelves of the libraries are full of other books, giving like proof. And, for that matter, this work is not written to convince people of the truth of this phenomena—it is intended for those who have at. ready convinced themselves of its reality, but who wish for specific information regarding its nature, manner of manifestation, etc. Where we quote instances of the manifestation of some form of Psychomantic phenomena, in this work, we do so simply to illustrate the characteristics of some particular form of the phenomena, and not as corroborative proof. With this explanation, we propose plunging right into the main subject itself.

There have been many attempted explanations of, and theories regarding the phenomena of Psychomancy, some of which are more or less plausible, while others are quite visionary, "wild," and fantastic. In this work, we shall pay no attention to those more or less ingenious "guesses" of the theorists, but shall, instead, give you plainly, clearly, and simply, the time-honored teachings of the advanced Occultists which teachings we believe to be the Truth, tested and tried by centuries of investigation, and experiment.

THE ASTRAL SENSES.

The Occult Teachings inform us that in addition to the Five Physical Senses possessed by man, viz: Seeing; Feeling; Hearing; Tasting; and Smelling; each of which has its appropriate sense organ, every individual is also possessed of Five Astral Senses, which form a part of what is known to Occultists as the Astral Body. These Astral Senses, which are the astral counterparts of the five physical senses, operate upon what Occultists call the Astral Plane, which is next above the Physical Plane, in the Sevenfold Scale of Planes. Just as do the Physical Senses operate upon the Physical Plane, so do the Astral Senses operate upon the Astral Plane.

By means of these Astral Senses, one may sense outside objects without the use of the physical senses usually employed. And it is through this sensing by these Astral Senses, that the phenomena of Psychomancy becomes possible.

By the employment of the Astral Sense of Seeing, the Psychomancer is able to perceive occurrences, scenes, etc., at a distance sometimes almost incredibly far; to see through solid objects; to see records of past occurrences in the Astral Ether; and to see Future Scenes thrown ahead in Time, like the shadows cast by material objects—"coming events cast their shadows before," you have heard. By the use of the Astral Sense of Hearing, he is able to sense sounds over immense distances and often after the passage of great periods of time, for the Astral vibrations continue for many years.

The Astral senses of Taste and Smell are seldom used, although there are abundant proofs of their existence. The Astral Sense of Feeling enables the Psychomancer to become aware of certain occurrences on the Astral Plane, and to perceive impressions, mental and otherwise, that are being manifested at a distance. The Astral Sense of Feeling may be explained as being rather a sense of "Awareness," than a mere "Feeling," in-as-much as the Psychomancer, through its channel, becomes "aware" of certain occurrences, other than by Astral Sight or Hearing, and yet which is not "Feeling" as the word is used on the Physical Plane. It may be well called "Sensing" for want of a better name, and manifests in a vague consciousness or "awareness." But still we must not overlook the fact that there are many instances of true "feeling" on the Astral Plane, for instances, cases where the Psychomancer actually "feels" the pain of another, which phenomena is commonly known as "sympathetic pains," "taking on the condition," etc., etc., and which are well known to all investigators as belonging to the phenomena of the Astral Senses.

THE ASTRAL BODY

But, to understand the Astral Senses, one must be made acquainted with the existence of that which Occultists know as "The Astral Body." There is no point in the Occult Teachings better established; longer held; or more thoroughly proven than that of the existence of the Astral Body. This teaching of the Ancient Occultists is being corroborated by the experiments, and investigations of the Psychic Researchers of the present day.

The Astral Body, belonging to every person, is an exact counterpart of the perfect physical body of the person. It is composed of fine ethereal matter, and is usually encased in the physical body. In ordinary cases, the detaching of the Astral Body from its physical counterpart is accomplished only with great difficulty, but in the case of dreams; great mental stress; and under certain conditions of occult development, the Astral Body may become detached and sent on long journeys, traveling at a rate of speed greater than that of light waves. On these journeys it is always connected with the physical body by a long filmy connecting link. If this link were to become broken, the person would die instantly, but this is an almost unheard of occurrence in the ordinary planes of action. The Astral Body exists a long time after the death of the physical body, but it disintegrates in time. It sometimes hovers around the resting place of the physical corpse, and is mistaken for the "spirit" of the deceased person, although really it is merely a shell or finer outer coating of the soul., The Astral Body of a dying person is often projected to the presence of friends and loved ones a few moments before the physical death, the phenomenon arising from the strong desire of the dying person to see and be seen.

The Astral Body frequently travels from its physical counterpart, in Psychomantic phenomena, and visits scenes far

9

distant, there sensing what is occurring. It also leaves the body during what are known as Psychomantic dreams; or under the influence of anesthetics; or in some of the deeper phases of hypnosis; when it visits strange scenes and places, and often holds mental conversation with other Astral Bodies, or else with disembodied entities. The jumbled and distorted recollections of these dreams are occasioned by the brain not having received perfect impressions transmitted to it, by reason of lack of training, development, etc., the result being like a blurred or distorted photographic plate.

In order to intelligently grasp the underlying principles of the phenomena of Psychomancy, and its allied subjects, you must familiarize yourself with the truth concerning the Astral Senses, which we have just stated. Unless you understand and accept this truth and fact, you will not be able to grasp the principles underlying the phenomena in question, but will be lost in the quagmire of idle theories, and fantastic "explanation" hazarded by investigators of psychic phenomena who have not made themselves acquainted with the Occult Teachings which alone give the student an intelligent key to the mysteries of the Astral Plane.

THE THREE CLASSES

The phenomena of Psychomancy, etc., may be grouped into three classes, each being produced by its own special class-cause. In either or all cases, the impressions are received by and through the Astral Senses, but there are three distinct ways in which, and by which, these impressions are received. These ways, which we shall now proceed to consider in detail, may be classified under the following terms:

(1)   Sensing by the "quickening" of one's Astral Senses sufficient to perceive more clearly the etheric vibrations or currents, the auric emanations of persons and things; and similar phases of Psychomancy, but which does not include the power to sense occurrences happening in distant places; nor the power to sense the records of the past, or to receive indications of the future. (See Lesson III.)

(2)   Sensing by means of the "Astral Tube," erected in the Ether by the operation of one's Will or Desire, and which acts as a Psychic "telescope," or "microscope," with "X Ray" features. (See Lesson IV.)

(3)   Sensing by means of the actual projection of one's own Astral Body to the distant scene. (See Lesson VII.)

CLAIRAUDIENCE.

"Clairaudience" is a term sometimes used to indicate Astral Hearing. Some writers on this subject treat "Clairaudience" as a separate class of phenomena. But we fail to see the distinction they make. It, of course, employs a different Astral Sense from that generally employed, but both are Astral Senses functioning on the Astral Plane, just as they physical senses of Seeing and Hearing function on the Physical Plane. And, more important, both forms of Astral Sensing are subject to the same laws and rules. In other words, all that is said in the lessons of this book on the subject of Psychomantic Vision holds equally true of Clairaudience.

Thus, there may be Simple **Clairaudience**; Space

Clairaudience; Past Time **Clairaudience**; Future Time **Clairaudience**, etc.; also **Clairaudient** Psychometry; **Clairaudience** through Crystal Gazing, etc. Psychomantic Vision is the employment of the Astral **Sight**, while Clairaudience is the similar employment of the Astral **Hearing**.

In many cases of Psychomantic Vision there is an accompaniment of Clairaudience; while in others it may be missing. Likewise, Psychomantic Vision usually accompanied Clairaudience, although sometimes one may be able to **hear** astrally, although no seeing.

You will notice that in many of the instances of Psychomantic Vision related in this book, there is a mention of the person **hearing** words or sounds, while seeing the vision—this, of course, is Clairaudience.

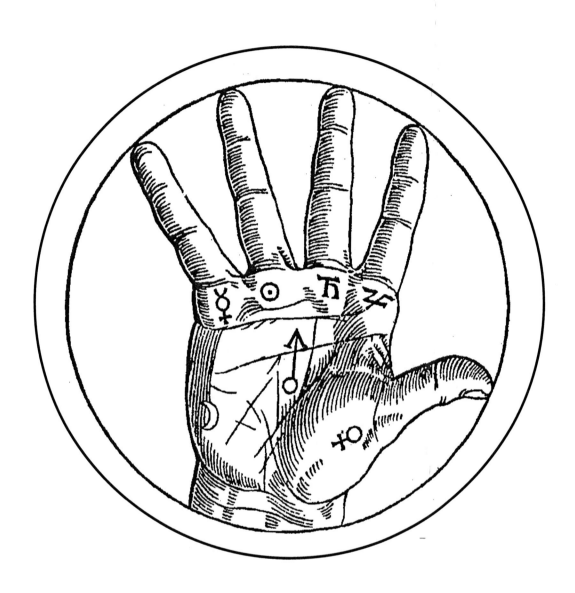

Lesson II.
How To Develop Yourself

PASSING to the actual practice, we desire to inform our students that 'the faculty of Psychomancy lies dormant in every person— that is the Astral Senses are present. in everyone, and the possibility of their being awakened into activity is always present. The different degrees of power observable in different persons depend chiefly upon the degree of development, or unfoldment, rather than upon the comparative strength of the faculties. In some persons,, of certain temperaments, the Astral Senses are very near the manifesting point at all times. Flashes of what are considered to be "intuition," premonitions, etc., are really manifestations of Psychomancy in some phase. In the 'case of other persons, on the other hand, the Astral Senses are almost atrophied, so merged in materialistic thought and life are these people. The element of Faith also plays an important point in this phenomena, as it does in all Occult phenomena, for that matter. That is to say, that one's belief tends to open up the latent powers and faculty in man, while a corresponding **disbelief** tends to prevent the unfoldment or manifestation. There is a very good psychological reason for this as all students of the subject well know. Belief and Disbelief are

15

two potent psychological factors on all planes of action.

Occultists know, and teach, that the Astral Senses and faculties of the human race will unfold as the race progresses, at which time that which we now call Psychomantic Power will be a common possession of all persons, just as the use of the Physical Senses are to the race at the present time. In the meantime, there are persons who, not waiting for the evolution of the race, are beginning to manifest this power in a greater or lesser degree, depending much upon favorable circumstances, etc. There are many more persons in this stage of development than is generally realized. In fact many persons manifesting Psychomantic power, occasionally, are apt to pass by the phenomena as "imagination," and "foolishness," refusing to recognize its reality. Then, again, many persons manifest the power during sleeping hours, and dismiss the matter as "merely a dream," etc.

Regarding this matter of the dawning of Psychomancy, a well-known authority writes as follows: "Students often ask how this psychic faculty will first be manifested in themselves—how they may know when they have reached the stage at which its first faint foreshadowings are beginning to be visible. Cases differ so widely that it is impossible to give to this question an answer that will be universally applicable. Some people begin by a plunge, as it were, and under some unusual stimulus become able just for once to see some striking vision; and very often in such a case, because the experience does not repeat itself, the seer comes in time to believe that on that occasion he must have been the victim of hallucination. Others begin by becoming intermittently conscious of the brilliant colors and vibrations of the human aura; others find themselves with increasing frequency seeing and hearing something to which those around them are blind and deaf; others again see faces, landscapes, or colored clouds floating before their eyes in the dark, before they sink to rest; while perhaps the commonest experience of all is that of those who begin to recollect with greater and greater clearness what they have seen and heard on other planes during sleep."

Very many persons possess respectable degrees of Simple Psychomancy, varying from vague impressions to the full manifestation of the faculty, as described in these lessons. Such a person has "intuitions"; "notions"; "presentiments," and the faculty of getting ideas regarding other persons and things, other than by the usual mental processes. Others manifest certain degrees of Psychometric powers, which develop rapidly by practice. Others find themselves possessing certain degrees of power of "scrying" through Crystals, which power, also, may be developed by practice. The phases of Time Psychomancy, Past and Future; and that of Space Psychomancy, in its higher degrees, are far more rare, and few persons possess them, and still fewer persist in the practice until they develop it, they lacking the patience, persistence, and application necessary.

While it is very difficult to lay down a set method of instruction in the Development of Psychomantic Power, owing to reasons already given, and because of the varying temperaments, etc., of students, yet there is possible a plan of giving general information, which if followed will put the student upon the right path toward future development. And this plan we I shall now proceed to give the students of this little book.

DEVELOPMENT METHODS

Concentration. In the first place, the student should cultivate the faculty of Concentration, that is the power to hold the attention upon an object for some time. Very few persons possess this power, although they may think they do. The best way to develop Concentration is to practice on some familiar and common object, such as **a** pencil, book, ornament, etc. Take up the object and study it in detail, forcing the mind to examine and consider it in every part, until every detail of the object has been observed and noted. Then lay the object aside, and a few hours after pick it up again and repeat the process, and you will be surprised to see how many points you have missed on the first trial, Repeat this until you feel that you have exhausted your object. The next day take up another object, and repeat tile process. A drill of this kind will not only greatly develop the powers of Perception, but will also strengthen your powers of Concentration in a manner which will be of great value to you in Occult Development.

Visualizing. The second point of development for the student, is the development of the faculty of Visualization. In order to Visualize you must cultivate the faculty of forming Mental Pictures of distant scenes, places, people, etc., until you can summon them before you at will, when you place yourself in the proper mental condition. Another plan is to place yourself in a comfortable position, and then make a mental journey to some place that you have previously visited. Prepare for the journey, and then mentally see yourself starting on your trip; then seeing all the intermediate places and points; then arriving at your destination and visiting the points of interest, etc.; and then returning home. Then, later try to visit places that you have never seen, in the same way. This is not Clairvoyance, but is a training of the mental faculties for the exercise of the real power.

Psychometry. After you have developed yourself along the lines of Concentration, and Visualization as above stated, you may begin to practice Psychometry, as follows: Take a lock of hair; or handkerchief; or ribbon; or ring; belonging to some other person, and then press it against your forehead, lightly, closing your eyes, and assuming a receptive and passive mental state.

Then desire calmly that you Psychometrize the past history of the object. Do not be in too much of a hurry, but await calmly the impressions. After a while you will begin to receive impressions concerning the person owning the object pressed against your forehead. You will form a mental picture of the person, and will soon begin to receive impressions about his characteristics, etc. You may practice with a number of objects, at different times, and will gradually develop the Psychometric power by such practice and experiments. Remember that you are developing what is practically a new sense, and must have perseverance and patience in educating and unfolding it.

Another form of Psychometric development is that of tracing the past history, surroundings, etc., of metals, minerals, etc. The process is identical to that just described. The mineral is pressed against the forehead, and with closed eyes the person awaits the Psychometric impression. Some who have highly developed the faculty have been able to describe the veins of mineral, metal, etc., and to give much valuable information regarding same, all arising from the psychic clue afforded by a sample of the rock, mineral, metal, etc. There are other cases of record, in which underground streams of water have been discovered by Psychometrists, by means of the clue given by a bit of earth, stone, etc., from the surface. In this, as in the other phase mentioned, **practice, practice, practice**, is the summing up of the instruction regarding development.

Crystal Gazing. We consider the use of the Crystal Glass Ball, or other forms of what the ancients called "The Magic Mirror," to be the best plan of developing Psychomantic Power.

As we have already explained, this method serves to focus the concentrated desire, will, and thought of the person, and thereby becomes the starting point for the Astral Tube, of which we have frequently spoken in this work. The student becoming proficient in this class of phenomena, passes by easy, gradual and natural stages to the higher and more complex phases of the subject. The "Magic Mirror" (of which the Crystal is but a form) was used by the ancient Occultists in developing the powers of their students, and in all countries, and in all ages, it has played a similar part in the process of developing psychic powers, and serving as a focal point for the erection and operation of the Astral Tube, in Psychomancy and other forms of occult and psychic phenomena.

At this point, we wish to tell you that there is no special virtue or magical properties or qualities in the Crystal itself—it is merely an instrument for Astral Vision, just as the telescope, microscope and other optical instruments are instruments employed in the phenomena of physical vision. It is true that the atomic and molecular characteristics of glass, crystal, etc., tend to produce the best results, but, after all, water, ink, etc., have been, and may be similarly used. No, there is no special "magic" in. the crystal itself, so do not allow yourself to fall into any superstition regarding its use.

Various teachers use different forms of the Crystal, or substitutes for it. Some of the teachers whose patrons are among the wealthier classes of the community, insist upon their pupils possessing globes of pure crystal, insisting that the latter alone gives the best results. But others who have pupils among people with shorter purses, have found that their pupils obtained just as good results by the use of a ball of plain glass, which is inexpensive. Others have advocated the use of watch crystals laid over a piece of black cloth, preferably velvet. Others have used polished steel objects, or pieces of polished metal of various kinds, a new silver coin, for instance. Others still have used a large drop of ink poured into a small dish, etc. Others have had cups painted black on their inner surface, into which they poured water, and claimed to have obtained the finest results. All the old talk about magic ceremonies and incantations being necessary in manufacturing the Magic Mirror, is pure nonsense, which has grown around the scientific facts of the case, as is so often the case. Do not be deceived by any such tomfoolery. A number of persons prefer to gaze into the bright substance of a precious stone. So you see, when we use the term "Crystal," we mean that the student may make his choice of any, or several, of the above-mentioned objects, or that he may even substitute some other object of his own choosing, possessing the requisite power of reflection.

There are but very few directions to be given in the use of the Crystal. Read what we have to say at the conclusion of our lesson on "Crystal Gazing" in this book, (Lesson VI). The principal point insisted upon by nearly all the teachers, is that Of placing the back of the gazer to the light, instead of having him face the light.

The simple general direction is that the gazer should practice by himself, at first, in a quiet room, sitting with his back toward the light, with the Crystal placed before him on a table, on a piece of black cloth, or other dark material, and then gaze calmly at the Crystal. Do not be afraid of winking, and do not strain or tire the eyes. Some prefer making funnels of their hands, and gazing through them just as if they were opera-glasses, and we think this plan a very good one, for it serves to shut out distracting light, and sights. If you fail to see anything at the first trial, do not be discouraged, but persevere. A number of trials are necessary in some cases, while in others wonderful results have been obtained at the first experiment.

An English authority recommends that beginners failing to get direct results, then try to "visualize" something that they have already seen — something familiar, such as a chair, a ring, a face, etc., and then turning to the Crystal endeavor to reproduce it there. It is claimed that this practice will often gradually lead to actual "seeing" in the Crystal.

The first signs of the actual "seeing" in the Crystal, comes in the form of a "cloudiness," or "milky-mist" in the crystal, which slowly resolves itself into a form, or scene, which appears gradually like the precipitation of a photograph upon a sensitive plate in the developing room. In some cases, the "misty" cloud deepens into a black one, from which the pictures appear.

General Advice. In this work we give you a comprehensive, although condensed, account of the various phases of the phenomena of Psychomancy, together with a number of instances of typical manifestations. By reading the following lessons, after having read the present one, the student will be able to gather much practical instruction on the subject of the manifestation of the power. He will be able to understand the nature and general workings of the phenomena, so that, when he undertakes the work of developing the power within himself, he will recognize the indication of his increasing power and unfolding faculties, which otherwise would "be Greek" to him. In order to get the very best results of instruction in this line, the student would of course do well to secure some competent instructor who could give him personal lessons. But, the person who has the patience and perseverance to "work the thing out for himself," as many before him have done, will obtain results none the less valuable because they were worked for without assistance.

We feel that we have given the students of this little work, such an idea of the general subject, and its fundamental laws, together with such general instruction in the methods of developing and manifesting the power that it will be one's own fault if he fails to get at least a fair degree of success from his undertaking self-development along these lines. There is no royal road to occult or psychic power — or "magic word" which when once pronounced will prove an "open Sesame" to the Doors of Psychomancy. And we would warn the student against persons who undertake to impart the "Secret" upon the payment of a goodly sum of money. There is no "Secret" to be so imparted — it is all a matter, first of general understanding, and then practice and work. To some it comes easier than to others, but even to such, the higher degrees mean work and practice. We trust that we have given you food for thought and material for practice. The rest depends upon yourself.

Lesson III.
Simple Psychomancy

THE phenomena of Psychomancy may be divided into three general classes, depending upon the nature of the "seeing," as follows:

I. Simple Psychomancy, by which is meant the power of "sensing" by means of the Astral Senses in the degree of a mere "quickening" of the Astral Senses sufficiently to enable one to "sense" more clearly any etheric vibrations or currents; the auric emanations of persons and things; and similar phases of Psychomantic phenomena; but which does not include the power to sense actual occurrences happening in distant places; nor the power to sense the records of the past, or to receive indications of the future.

II. Space Psychomancy, by which is meant the power to sense **distant** scenes, persons, or objects.

III. Time Psychomancy, by which is meant the power to sense objects, events, persons, etc., in the records of the past;

and also the power to sense the indications of the future—the "shadows of coming events."

Simple Psychomancy is very much more common than is generally supposed. Very many people are quite sensitive to "impressions" coming to them in this way, which while akin to. the impressions of Telepathy, nevertheless belong to the higher grade of Psychic Phenomena known as Psychomancy. It may be well to state here the difference between ordinary Telepathic impressions, and those of Simple Psychomancy. Many students are perplexed by the similarity between the two mentioned classes of phenomena, and we think it advisable to set them straight regarding the matter, at this point.

As we have stated in our previous work in this series, (entitled "Practical Mind Reading") Telepathy is occasioned by the passage of Thought Waves or Currents, passing from one brain to another, just as pass the waves of Heat, Light, Electricity, etc. In Telepathy the brain of the Transmitter sends forth the vibration, waves, or currents, and the brain of the Receiver registers the same, receiving them by means of the Pineal Gland which acts in a manner closer resembling that of the receiving instrument in Wireless Telegraphy. In Telepathy there is merely the sending and receiving of thought vibrations, **over the physical organs.**

But in Simple Psychomancy, the person may, and does, receive the thought vibrations emanating from the mind of another, but not over the physical channels, as in Telepathy, **but by means of the Astral Senses.** In this lies the difference.

Now, it follows that the Astral Senses being far more keen and acute than the Physical Senses, the former will register vibrations and impressions far more readily than the latter, and will often register impressions that the Physical Senses (even the

Pineal Gland organ) take no account of. In this way the person in whom the Astral Senses are even partially developed will receive impressions of the thoughts of others that even the most acute Mind Reader will fail to notice; as well as words actually spoken by the other person; and ideas forming in the mind of the other person not yet expressed in active thought-waves.

But, it should be added, the development of Telepathic powers very frequently grow into a development of Psychomantic powers, and so the former is one of the easiest paths to the latter, and may be used in developing Clairvoyant power, and in unfolding the Astral Senses. In this way the person possessing even a moderate degree of Psychomantic power often "feels" the thoughts, ideas, emotions, and other mental states of the people around him, and knows without any words being used just what the others are thinking and feeling. This is often perceived by merely the increased power to receive and register the Thought-vibrations, but in some cases the ability to sense the "Aura" of the other persons heighten the impression.

THE AURA

The majority of our readers are familiar with the fact that all persons, and objects, are surrounded by an emanation called an "Aura," or egg-shaped psychic emanation extending several feet around them. This aura is charged with the thought-vibrations of the persons, and is really the "atmosphere" that we feel surrounding people and by which we feel attracted or repelled as the case may be. The trained and developed Psychomancer is able to see the colors by which the various emotions, thoughts, etc., are indicated, but even when that degree of power is lacking, he may "feel" the general character of the various component parts of the person's aura.

While it is not our intention to go deeply into this matter of Auric Colors, in this work, still we think it well to indicate the same here, by quoting from a well-known authority on the subject, who says: "As he looks at a person he will see him surrounded by the luminous mist of the astral aura, flashing with all sorts of brilliant colors, and constantly changing in hue and brilliancy with every variation of the person's thoughts and feelings. He will see this aura flooded with the beautiful rose-color of pure affection; the rich blue of devotional feeling; the hard dull brown of selfishness; the deep scarlet of anger; the horrible lurid red of sensuality; the livid grey of fear; the black clouds of hatred and malice; or any of the other hundredfold indications so easily to be read in it by a practiced eye; and thus it will be impossible for any persons to conceal from him the real state of their feelings on any subject."

But only a comparatively few are able to distinctly see these Auric Colors, by reason of their lack of development along these special lines. But a great number of people are able to feel the subtle vibrations which give rise to these colors. Just as there are well authenticated cases of blind men and women being able to distinguish by the sense of feeling (in touch) the various colors which their blind eyes fail to see, so are thousands of people able to feel the auric shades which their imperfectly developed clairvoyant vision fails to perceive. In this connection it is interesting to note that science informs us that the sense of Feeling was the first developed of any of the physical senses; in fact all the other senses are developments of, and extensions of, the original sense of Feeling. And there is a close correspondence between this phenomena of the Physical Senses, and that of the Astral Senses.

But there are other, and perhaps more wonderful, features of Simple Psychomancy. It is a well established scientific fact that nearly, if not indeed all, objects are constantly emanating streams of Radiant Energy, or Streams of Electrons as they are called by some. The delicate instruments of science are able to detect and register some of the coarser vibrations of this energy, but the more delicate ones have so far escaped them. But the Astral Senses of the developed Psychomancer register and record many of the finer vibrations, and in this way many so-called "miracles" of occultism are explained. Let us examine this phenomena at this point.

It becomes apparent to any student of the subject, early in his investigations, that the Psychomancer is able to "see" things hidden by other objects, and often surrounded by the densest matter. In other words he is able to **see through solid objects**— to see "through a brick wall" to use the familiar phrase. Now this may seem almost incredible to one at the first mention of the subject. But when the skeptic's attention is called to the fact that the "X Rays" and similar forms of energy recently discovered by science, readily pierce through solid objects, and may be actually "seen" by the eye (aided by the proper instruments), or recorded on a photographic plate — then the impossible feat of "seeing though a brick wall" becomes a very simple, understandable matter, indeed. And in an almost identical manner the Psychomancer **sees through solid object—and the most solid material becomes transparent to his Astral Sight.**

The fine streams or waves of energy constantly being emanated by all objects, which are invisible to the naked physical eye, are registered and recorded by the Astral Sense of Sight. The Psychomancer even by means of the comparatively elementary power of Simple Psychomancy is able to see what is going on in an adjoining room, or other nearby place; to read the contents of a sealed letter; to describe the contents of a locked, steel book; or to read a chosen passage in a closed book.

To the developed and trained Psychomancer, when he concentrates his power, the solid ground over which he is walking, becomes transparent, and he is able to see down into its depths to a considerable distance. In this way he may see living underground creatures at work, and play; and to discover veins of mineral, coal, etc., or underground streams of water. In these cases the Clairvoyant **does not travel** in the Astral, but merely receives and perceives the subtle vibrations or streams of fine energy constantly being emanated by the objects. Some Clairvoyants have developed certain other less common faculties of Astral Sight, which give the "telescopic" and "microscopic" vision in these cases, in addition to the main faculty of "seeing" things through solid coverings.

The question will naturally arise in the mind of the student, whether there is any limit to the depths open to the Astral Sight of the Psychomancer (in this phase of the phenomena), as for instance when he is looking into the solid earth.

It may be urged that as objects at immense distances underground emanate rays just as truly as do objects nearer the surface, then there should be no difference in the power of vision. Answering this question we would say that the same objection and obstacle arises in this case, as in the corresponding physical phenomena, such as the X Rays. While a far distant object emits rays just as well as a nearby one, still there is **a** loss of energy according to distance, and the Astral Sense, like the Physical Sense, fails to clearly register after a certain distance is attained. This distance varies in the case of different persons using their Astral Vision, just as it does in the case of the different degrees of eyesight possessed by various persons. And then again, it must not be supposed that the earth becomes as clear as glass to the

Astral Vision. On the contrary it presents a similar appearance to that obtained when one is seeing objects through water or mist, with the physical eye. One can see quite a way through water or mist with the physical eye, but after a certain distance the impressions grow dim, and finally fade from view. Of course in the case of the erecting of the Astral Tube better results may be obtained, but this phenomena belongs to the class of Space Psychomancy.

There is another power open to the Psychomancer along the lines of Simple Psychomancy. We refer to the phenomena of "seeing into" the physical bodies of other people; examining the internal organs; diagnosing diseases, etc. Of course, in this case, before the Clairvoyant is able to correctly diagnose a disease he must be acquainted with the nature of the organs, and their appearance in their normal state, etc., so that he will recognize a diseased condition when he sees it. One must needs have an acquaintance with Anatomy and Physiology, as well as possessing trained Psychomantic powers for this work.

Lesson IV.
The Astral Tube.

THE term, "**The Astral Tube,**" is frequently with in the writings of Occultists, but you will find very little more than a mention of it in many of such works, the proverbial caution of the older writers having acted in the direction of preventing their entering into a fuller description or explanation, for fear of the information falling into improper hands. This will be more readily understood, when we tell you that the Astral Tube is, and may be, used for classes of phenomena other than that of Psychomancy, notably that of Mental Influencing, "treating", etc., which however forms no part of the present work, but which will be discussed in a future volume of the series to be called "Mental Influence, etc."

The Astral Plane is composed of an ethereal form of matter, very much rarer and finer than the matter of the Physical Plane—but matter, nevertheless, and subject to fired laws and conditions. And, just as it is possible to establish "lines of force" in the physical matter, so may corresponding "lines of force" be established in Astral matter. And this Astral Tube is really such a "line of force." In other words, it is possible to set up and establish a "line of force" on the Astral Plane, that will serve as a ready conductor of Astral vibrations, currents, etc., and which affords a highly efficient channel of communication between objects far removed from each other in space. And this channel is actually created and used in a variety of forms of Occult phenomena.

POLARIZATION.

You have heard of "Polarity," and "Polarization" in connection with electrical phenomena. "Polarity" is defined by Webster as: "That quality or condition of a body by virtue of which it exhibits opposite or contrasted properties or powers, in opposite or contrasted parts or directions; or, a condition giving rise to a contrast of properties corresponding to a contrast of positions." And, "Polarization" is defined by the same authority as: "Act of polarizing; state of have polarity." Well, then, the process of erecting the Astral Tube is practically that of the "polarization" of the particles of Astral matter by an effort of the human Will, set in motion by means of a strong Desire or Determination, under certain conditions.

When the human Will is directed toward a distant person or object, under the proper psychic conditions, it tends to "polarize" a path or channel through the Astral atmosphere toward the desired point, which channel becomes at once an easy course of psychic communication for the transmission or receiving of psychic impressions or expressions, as the case may be. And, in the case of Psychomancy and kindred phenomena, the Astral Senses of the person (even though his Astral Body be still within its physical counterpart) are able to readily "sense" the impressions being manifested at a far distant point in space.

The above mentioned channel of communication—the Astral Tube — has not of course the advantages of actual travel in the Astral Body, and is besides affected by certain Astral happenings, such as the breaking up of the tube, or an impairment of its efficiency, by reason of some stronger astral current or channel, etc., for instance. When one considers the currents and cross-currents constantly in operation on the Astral Plane, it will be seen how likely the above mentioned interference is to happen.

Through the Astral Tube the Astral Senses actually "sense' 'the sights, and often the sounds being manifested at a distance, just as one may see distant sights through a telescope, or hear distant sounds through a telephone, for instance. It also may be used as a microscope, as we shall see as we proceed. The student's attention is especially directed toward the fact that in this form of phenomena, the Psychomancer remains within his physical body, and does not travel in the Astral at all. He sees the distant scenes, just as a man sees them through a telescope. His consciousness remains within his physical body.

A well known writer on this subject has truly said: "...the limitations resemble those of a man using a telescope on the physical plane. The experimenter, for example, has a particular field of view which cannot be enlarged or altered; he is looking at his scene from a certain direction, and he cannot suddenly turn it all around and see how it looks from the other side. If he has sufficient psychic energy to spare, he may drop altogether the telescope that he is using, and manufacture an entirely new one for himself which will approach his objective somewhat differently; but, this is not a course at all likely to be adopted in practice. But it may be said, the mere fact that he is using Astral Sight ought to enable him to see it from all sides at once. And so it would, if he were using that sight in the normal way upon an object which was fairly near him—within his astral reach as it were; but at a distance of hundreds or thousands of miles the case is very different. Astral sight gives us the advantage of an additional dimension, but there is still such a thing as position in that dimension, and it is naturally a potent factor in limiting the use of the powers of its plane.

...Astral sight, when it is cramped by being directed along what is practically a tube, is limited very much as physical sight would be under similar circumstances, though if possessed in perfection it will continue to show, even at that distance, the auras, and therefore all the emotions and most of the thoughts of the people under observation."

The Astral Tube, in connection with Psychomancy, is used in a variety of forms. It is often used unconsciously, and springs into existence spontaneously, under the power of some strong emotion, desire or will. It is also observed in some cases of hypnotic phenomena, in which the hypnotist uses his will to cause his subject to form an Astral Tube, and then report his impressions. It is also used by the trained Psychomancer, without the use of any "starting point," or "focal centre," simply by the exercise of his trained, developed and concentrated will. But its most familiar and common use is in connection with some object serving as a "starting point," or "focal centre."

The "starting point" or "focal centre," above mentioned, is generally either what is known as "the associated object" in the class of phenomena commonly known as "Psychometry," or else a glass or crystal-ball, or' similar polished reflecting surface, in what is known as "Crystal Gazing." In the two next succeeding lessons, we shall consider these two forms of phenomena, respectively.

Lesson V.
Psychometry

THE phenomena commonly known as "Psychometry," is but one phase of Psychomancy — or it even may be said to be but a **method employed** to bring into action the Astral Senses. The Psychometrist merely **gets into rapport** with the distant scene; or period of time; or person; or object; by using some bit of physical material associated with that scene; time; person; objects; etc., in order to "open up communications" along the usual lines of Psychomancy. This has been compared to the use of objects associated with a thing in the case of memory. We all know how the sight of some object will recall at once memories of things long since forgotten to all appearances, but which memories have been merely stored away in the great storehouse of the mind, to 'be recalled readily when the "association" is furnished. What "association" is in the case of Memory, so is the material object presented as the "associated object" in Psychometry.

The Occult Teachings inform us that **there is a psychic**

connection ever existing between things once associated, and that when we throw ourselves into the psychic current surrounding an object we may readily follow the current back until we reach the associated object for which we are seeking on the Astral Plane. In the Akashic Records (See Lesson IX) all memories are registered and recorded, and if we have a good starting point we may travel back until we find that which we desire, In the same way the "associated object" furnishes us with a ready means of starting our Astral Tube into being and use. This is the secret of the use of the lock of hair; the bit of clothing; the piece of metal or mineral, etc., used by Psychometrists.

A well known authority on the subject has said concerning Psychometry: "It may be asked how it is possible, amid the bewildering confusion of these records of the past, to find any particular picture when it is wanted. As a matter of fact, the untrained psychic usually cannot do so without some special link to put him in rapport with the subject required. Psychometry is an instance in point, and it is quite probable that our ordinary memory is really only another presentment of the same idea. It seems as though there were a sort of magnetic attachment or affinity between any particle of matter and the record which contains its history — and affinity which enables it to act as **a** kind of conductor between that record and the faculties of anyone who can read it. For instance, I once brought from Stonehenge a tiny fragment of stone, not larger than a pin's head, and on putting this into an envelope and handing it to a psychometrist who had no idea what it was, she at once began to describe the wonderful ruin from which it came, and the desolate country surrounding it, and then went on to picture vividly what were evidently scenes from its early history, showing that the infinitesimal fragment had been sufficient to put her into communication with the records connected with the spot from which it came. The scenes through which we pass in the course of our life seem to act in the same manner upon the cells of our brain as did the history of

Stonehenge upon that particle of stone; they establish a connection with those cells by means of which our mind is put in rapport with that particular portion of the records, and so we 'remember' what we have seen."

THE FIVE METHODS

The method of Psychometry may be employed in a number of ways, among which are the following, all of which are subject to many variations and combinations:

1. Locating a person by means of a lock of hair, article of clothing, handkerchief, ribbon, piece of jewelry, bit of writing, etc. In this manner not only may a good Psychometrist locate the person, but will also be able to give an idea of his characteristics, habits, health, etc.

2. Describing a person's characteristics, past life, future, etc., by means of the rapport condition made possible by the person's presence.

3. Describing a present distant scene by means of a bit of mineral, plant, or similar object once located at the place.

4. Describing the surrounding underground characteristics by means of a bit of mineral, etc.

5. Getting into touch with the past history Of an object, or its surroundings, by means of the object itself. For instance, a bullet from the battle-field may give the history of the battle; a bit of ancient pottery, the

characteristics and habits of the people who made or used it, as well as the appearance of the land in which they dwell, etc.

In all of these phases, with their variations and combination, the student will see the operation of the phenomena under the various heads as classified by us in this work. Each Occurrence or manifestation will be found to fit into the class of Simple Psychomancer; Space Psychomancy; Past Time Psychomancy; or Future Time Psychomancy.

(See Lesson II, for suggestions regarding development of Psychometric power.)

Lesson VI.
Crystal Gazing

THERE has been a great revival of interest in the subject of "Crystal Gazing," particularly in England, of late years, and many interesting accounts have appeared in the papers and magazines regarding the results of the experiments. But the majority of the writers on the subject persist in treating it as a thing separate and apart from other forms of Psychomancy— in fact, many of them ignore Psychomancy altogether and are apparently under the impression that there is no connection between it and their favorite subject of Crystal Gazing. This attitude is somewhat amusing to persons who have made a careful study of Psychic Phenomena and who know that Crystal Gazing is not a distinct phenomenon, but is merely a method of bringing into action the Psychomantic faculties.

In many respects the Crystal acts in a manner akin to that of the "associated object" in Psychometry, but there is one point of distinction which should not be overlooked by the student. The "associated object" gives to the Psychometrist a **starting point for the Astral Tube**, and also serves to "point the Astral Telescope" (if one may use the term) in the right direction, by

41

reason of its affinity with the distant scene, etc. But the Crystal does not so act, for it is not closely allied to, or in sympathy with other things, when used in the ordinary manner. Instead of being the "eye-lens of the telescope," it is really a "Magic Mirror" which is turned first this way and that, and which reflects whatever comes within its field, just as does any other mirror. The trained and developed Psychomancer, however, may direct his Mirror to any desired point, and may hold it there by means of a concentrated Will.

The favor with which Crystal Gazing meets with at the hands of beginners is due to the fact that it is the easiest method known by which the Astral Vision may be awakened. With the majority of people, the power may be awakened only by the aid of some physical object which may act as a starting-point for the Astral Tube, or as one writer has expressed it, "a convenient focus for the Will-power." A number of objects may be so employed, but the Crystal or Glass Ball is the best for the purpose because of certain atomic and molecular arrangements which tend to promote the manifestation of the psychic power and faculties.

Crystal Gazing, as a method for inducing Psychomantic vision, has been quite common among all peoples, in all times. Not only the Crystal but many other objects are similarly used. In Australia the native priests use water and shining objects, or in some cases, flame. In New Zealand some of the natives use a drop of blood. The Fijians fill a hole with water, and gaze into it. Some South American tribes use the polished surface of a black stone. The American Indians used water and shining bits of flint or quartz. And so the story goes. As Lang states it, people "stare into a crystal ball; a cup; a mirror; a blot of ink (Egypt and India); a drop of blood (the Maoris of New Zealand); a bowl of water (American Indians); a pond (Roman and African); water in a glass bowl (Fez); or almost any polished surface, etc."

Crystal Gazing

We quote a typical case of Crystal Gazing, related by Mr. Andrew Lang. He says:

"I had given a glass ball to a young lady, Miss Baillie, who had scarcely any success with it. She lent it to Miss Leslie, who saw a large, square, old-fashioned red sofa covered with muslin (which she afterward found in the next country-house she visited). Miss Baillie's brother, a young athlete, laughed at these experiments, took the ball into his study, and came back looking 'gey gash.' He admitted that he had seen a vision—somebody he knew, under a lamp. He said he would discover during the week whether he saw right or not. This was at 5:30 on a Sunday afternoon. On Tuesday, Mr. Baillie was at a dance in a town forty miles from his home, and met a Miss Preston. 'On Sunday,' he said, 'about half-past five, you were sitting under a standard lamp, in a dress I never saw you wear, a blue blouse with lace over the shoulders, pouring out tea for a man in blue serge, whose back was towards me, so that I only saw the tip of his moustache.' 'Why, the blinds must have been up,' said Miss Preston. 'I was at Dulby,' said Mr. Baillie, and he undeniably was."

Stead relates the following experience with the Crystal: "Miss X. upon looking into the crystal on two occasions as a test, to see if she could see men when she was several miles off, saw not me, but a different friend of mine on each occasion. She had never seen either of my friends before, but immediately identified them both on seeing them afterward at my office. On one of the evenings on which we experimented in the vain attempts to photograph a Double, I dined with Madam C. and her friend at a neighboring restaurant. As she glanced at the water bottle, Madame C. saw a picture beginning to form, and, looking at it from curiosity, described with considerable detail an elderly gentleman whom she had never seen before, and whom I did not in the least recognize from her description at the moment. Three hours afterwards, when the séance was over, Madam C. entered the room and recognized Mr. Elliott, of Messrs. Elliott & Fry, as the gentleman whom she had seen and described in the water bottle at the restaurant. On another occasion the picture was less agreeable: it was an old man lying dead in bed with some one weeping at his feet; but who it was, or what it related to, no one knew."

As a matter of general interest, we also quote Mr. Stead's remarks on crystal gazing, which agree with our own views and experience. He says:

"There are some people who cannot look into an ordinary globular bottle without seeing pictures form themselves, without any effort, or will on their part, in the crystal globe. Crystal gazing seems to be the least dangerous and most simple of all forms of experimenting. You simply look into a crystal globe the size of a five-shilling piece, or a water bottle which is full of clear water, and which is placed so that too much light does not fall upon it, and then simply look at it. You make no incantations, and engage in no mumbo-jumbo business; you simply look at it for two or three minutes, taking care not to tire yourself, winking as much as you please, but fixing your thought upon whatever you wish to see. Then, if you have the faculty, the glass will cloud over with a milky mist, and in the centre the image is gradually precipitated in just the same way as a photograph forms on the sensitive plate."

(See Lesson II, for further particulars on Crystal Gazing, and suggestions for the successful development of the power.)

Lesson VII.
Astral Projection

IN OUR last three lessons we considered that class of Psychomancy arising from the erection and employment of the "Astral Tube." In the present lesson we pass to a consideration of the third class of phenomena, namely, that occasioned by the actual projection of one's Astral Body to distant points.

In this class of phenomena the consciousness of the person does not remain within the physical organism, but is actually projected along with the Astral Body to the point being psychically viewed or examined. This form of Psychomancy is, of course, a higher degree of manifestation than the class previously described. Here physical consciousness is temporarily suspended (perhaps for but a moment or so) and the Astral Body containing the consciousness of the individual is projected to some point, perhaps far distant, with the rapidity of thought, where it examines objects there situated, receiving sensations through and by means of the Astral Senses. This phenomena may

47

arise while the person is in a trance, or sleep, etc., or else in a moment of concentrated abstraction, when one is "day-dreaming"; in a "brown study"; or "wrapped in thought," as the familiar terms run. When he returns to his physical body he "comes to himself," and what he has seen or heard seems to him like a "day-dream" or fantasy— unless he be a trained seer, in which case the two planes of consciousness will be closely related, and almost continuous.

Besides the more familiar phases of this class of phenomena, there are wonderful possibilities open for the developed Psychomancer along these lines. As a leading writer on this subject has said concerning it: "He has also the immense advantage of being able to take part, as it were, in the scenes which come before his eyes. If, in addition, he can learn how to materialize himself, he will be able to take part in physical events or conversations at a distance, and to show himself to an absent friend at will."

The trained experimenter along these lines has also the advantage of being able to search about on the Astral Plane for what he desires to find or locate. He is able to direct his Astral Body to definite places, either by means similar to finding one's way on the physical plane, or else by following up the psychic clue afforded by a piece of clothing, a lock of hair, a piece of stone, or some other object connected with the person or place desired, by means of a higher form of Psychometry. Of course, the person whose powers are not so highly developed is not able to have such control over his Astral Body, or to manifest such a degree of trained power. He is like a child learning to walk, or read —he is awkward, and must learn to direct his movements. There are many degrees of power, from the occasional, spontaneous manifestations, to those of the highly trained Occultists who travel in the Astral even more easily than in the physical, and with the same degree of certainty and control.

The pages of reliable works on Occultism and Psychic Research are filled with illustrations and examples of cases along these lines, in which the Astral Body of persons have traveled to distant scenes, and have reported occurrences and scenes witnessed there, sometimes materializing so as to be seen by the persons in the places visited. We herewith mention a few of these cases, in order to illustrate the principle.

A well-known example is that of the Philadelphian, mentioned by the German writer Jung Stilling, and quoted by some English writers. The man in question was a well-known character, respected, of good reputation and steady habits. He had the reputation of possessing Psychomantic powers which he sometimes manifested for the benefit of friends and others. He was once consulted by the wife of a sea captain, whose husband was on a voyage to Europe and Africa, and whose vessel had been long overdue, and from whom no tidings had been received for a long time.

The Psychomancer listened to the story of the anxious and distressed wife, and then excused himself from the room for a short time, retiring into an adjoining room. Becoming alarmed at his continued absence from the room, the lady quietly opened the connecting door, and peeped in the second room, where much to her surprise and alarm she saw the old man lying on a couch, showing all the appearances of death. She waited in great alarm for a long time, when he aroused himself and returned to her. He told her that he had visited her husband in a coffee-house in London, and gave her the reasons for his not having written, adding that he would soon return to Philadelphia.

When the husband finally returned, his wife questioned him regarding the matter, and he informed her that the reasons given by the Psychomancer were correct in every detail. Upon being taken into the presence of the man, the old sea captain uttered an exclamation of surprise, saying that he had seen the man on a certain day in a coffee-house in London, and that the man had told him that his wife was worried about him, and that he had answered the man, saying that he had been prevented from writing for certain reasons, and that he was on the very eve of setting sail for America. He said that he had then lost sight of the stranger suddenly.

W. T. Stead relates the case of a lady of his acquaintance who has spontaneously developed the power to travel in her Astral Body, and to materialize the same unconsciously. She became a source of great worry and distress to many of her friends, to whom she would pay unexpected and involuntary visits, frightening them out of their wits by the materialization of what they supposed must be the "ghost" of the lady, whom they thought must have died suddenly. The occurrences, however, became so frequent that her friends at last became familiar with the nature of the appearances, and viewed them with merely great interest and wonder.

The English Society for Psychical Research have several hundred well-authenticated instances of such appearances m their published records. One of the well-known cases is that of a gentleman described as "S. H. B.," a member of the London Stock Exchange, and a man of considerable business note. He relates his story as follows:

"One Sunday night in November, 1881, I was in Kildare Gardens, when I willed very strongly that I would visit in the spirit two lady friends, the Misses V., who were living three miles off, in Hogarth Road. I willed that I should do this at one o'clock in the morning, and having willed it, I went to sleep. Next Thursday, when. I first met my friends, the elder lady told me she woke up and saw my apparition advancing to her bedside. She screamed and woke her sister, who also saw me." (A signed statement of the two sisters accompanies this statement, both ladies fixing the time at one o'clock, and saying that Mr. B. wore evening dress.)

"Again, on December 1, 1882, I was at Southall. At half-past nine I sat down to endeavor to fix my mind so strongly upon the interior of a house at Kew, where Miss V. and her sister lived, that I seemed to be actually in the house. I was conscious, but was in a kind of mesmeric sleep. When I went to bed that night, I willed to be in the front bedroom of that house at Kew at twelve, and to make my presence felt by the inmates. Next day I went to Kew. Miss V.'s married sister told me, without any prompting from me, that she had seen me in the passage going from one room to another at half-past nine o'clock, and that at twelve, when she was wide awake, she saw me come to the front bedroom, where she slept, and take her hair, which is very long, into my hand. She said I then took her hand and gazed into the palm intently. She said, 'You need not look at the lines, for I never had any trouble.' She then woke her sister. When Mrs. L. told me this. I took out the entry that I had made the previous night and read it to her. Mrs. L. is quite sure she was not dreaming. She had only seen me once before, two years previously, at a fancy ball."

"Again, on March 22, 1884, I wrote to Mr. Gurney, of the Psychical Research Society, telling him I was going to make my presence felt by Miss V., at 44 Norland Square, at midnight. Ten days afterwards, I saw Miss V., when she voluntarily told me that on Saturday at midnight, she distinctly saw me, when she was quite wide awake."

We have related these accounts in order to show instances of the appearance of a materialized Astral Body. But, we must remember that these cases of materialization are very rare as compared to the cases of Astral Projection (without materialization) in ordinary Clairvoyance. And yet the phenomena is practically the same in both instances, leaving out the phase of materialization. In many instances the individual actually travels in his Astral Body to the distant scene and there witnesses the events occurring at that point. There is a "ghost" within each one of us, which under certain favorable conditions travels away from our physical body and "sees things" at far-off points. Under certain other conditions it materializes, and is visible to others, but in the majority of cases it merely "sees" without being seen. The Psychomancer, in this phase of the phenomena, actually travels from the location of the physical body, to the other points desired, and reports what he or she sees and hears there.

Astral Projection is frequently developed by faithful practice of, and demonstration of, the simpler forms of Psychomancy. It is all a matter of successive steps of development.

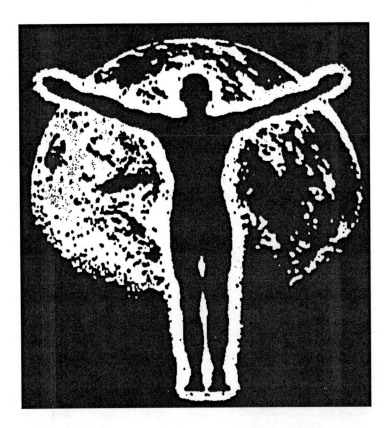

Lesson VIII.
Space Psychomancy

AS WE stated in previous lessons, "Space Psychomancy" is the exercise of the faculty in the direction of perceiving far-distant scenes, persons, objects, etc. Of course, there is really an exercise of Space Psychomancy in some instances of Simple Psychomancy. But we make the distinction because in the case of objects seen by Simple Psychomancy at some little distance from the observer, the impression is received by means of the rays, or vibrations from the objects themselves, by means of the developed Astral Senses, acting in a simple manner; while in the case of Space Psychomancy (in the technical sense of the term) the impression is received by means of either the erection of the Astral Tube, or else by the actual projection of the consciousness in the Astral Body — the latter being an actual visiting of the scene.

A little illustration may perhaps make clearer the above distinction. Let us suppose a man on the physical Plane with ordinary eyesight —such a man could not see an object beyond the average distance of vision, and he would be like a person devoid of Psychomantic powers.

Then let us suppose a man of extraordinary visual powers, such as many hunters or seafaring men — such a one could see things invisible to the first man, and would thus resemble the person manifesting Simple Psychomancy. Then let us suppose a third man, using a telescope —this man could see things that neither of the other two could perceive, and he would thus resemble the person manifesting along the lines of Space Psychomancy by means of the Astral Tube. And, finally, let us suppose a fourth man, who possessed magical wings which would instantly transport him to the distant scene, whence he could view the objects, personally, and at close range — well this man would be like the person who was able to project his Astral Body, and thus view the distant scenes at will, and at short range, without the difficulties attendant upon the use of the telescope-like Astral Tube — to see the object on any and all sides, and from all points of view — to get inside of it, as well as outside.

The following interesting cases are quoted to illustrate the principle:

Captain Yount, of the Napa Valley, California, had a peculiar experience while asleep. He had a remarkably clear vision in which appeared a band of emigrants perishing from cold and hunger amidst a mountain range. He noted particularly, and in detail, the scenery and appearance of the canyon. He saw a huge, perpendicular cliff of white rock; and the emigrants cutting off what appeared to be the tops of trees arising from great drifts of snow; he even saw plainly the features of some of the party. He awoke, sorely distressed by the vividness and the nature of his "dream," for so he considered it to be. But, by-and-by, he fell asleep again, and saw the scene repeated, with equal distinctness. In the morning he found that he could not get the "dream" out of his mind, and he told it to some of his friends. One of the hearers of the story was an old hunter, who at once recognized the place seen in the dream as a place across the

Sierras, known as a point in the Carson Valley Pass. So earnest was the old hunter, that Captain Yount, and his friends, organized a rescue party and set out with provisions, mules, and blankets to seek the perishing emigrants. Notwithstanding the ridicule of the public, the rescuers persisted in their search, and finally about one hundred and fifty miles distant, in the Carson Valley Pass, they found the scene as described by Captain Yount, and **in the identical spot seen in the dream were found the party of emigrants**, the surviving members of whom were rescued and brought over the mountain.

Another interesting account is given in the reports of the Society for Psychical Research, of England. It relates that an English lady, Mrs. Broughton, awoke one night in 1844, and aroused her husband, telling him that she had had a strange vision of a scene in France. She stated that she had seen a broken-down carriage, evidently wrecked in an accident, and a crowd gathered around the figure of a man, whose body was then raised and carried into a nearby house. She said that the body was then placed in a bed, when she recognized his features as those of the Duke of Orleans. Then friends gathered around the bed, and later came the king and queen of France, all weeping. She saw the doctor, who stood over the Duke, feel-bag his pulse, with his watch in his other hand, but she could only see the doctor's back. Then the scene had faded from her vision. When daylight finally came, she recorded the vision in her journal. It was before the days of the telegraph, and it was more than two days before the newspapers announced the death of the Duke of Orleans. The lady visited Paris afterwards, and recognized the place of the accident. It then appeared that the attending physician whose face she could not see in her vision, was an old friend of hers, who then told her that as he watched the bed his mind had involuntarily dwelt upon her and her family.

The well-known case of Swedenborg gives us another illustration of this class of Psychomancy. It is related that in the latter part of September, 1759, at four o'clock one Saturday afternoon, Swedenborg arrived home from England, and disembarked at Gothenburg. Mr. W. Castel met him and invited him to dinner, at which meal there were fifteen persons gathered around the table. At six o'clock that evening Swedenborg went out a few minutes, returning to the table excited and pale. When questioned, he said that there was a fire at Stockholm, 200 miles distant, which was steadily spreading. He grew very restless, and frequently left the room. He said that the house of one of his friends, whose name he mentioned, was already in ashes, and that his own was in danger. At eight o'clock after he had been out again, he returned crying out cheerfully, "Thank heaven! the fire is out, the third door from my house."

The news of the occurrence excited the whole town, and the officials made inquiry regarding it, and Swedenborg was summoned before the governor, and requested to relate what he had seen, in detail. Answering the governor, he told when and where the fire had started; how it had begun; how, when and where it had stopped; and the time it lasted, the number of houses destroyed, people injured, etc. On the following Monday morning a courier arrived from Stockholm, bringing news of the fire, having left the town while it was still burning. On the next day after, Tuesday morning, another courier arrived at the governor's palace with a full report of the fire, which corresponded precisely with the vision of Swedenborg—the fire had stopped precisely at eight o'clock, the minute that Swedenborg had so announced it to . the company.

Stead relates the following instance of this class of Psychomancy, which was told him by the wife of a Dean of the Episcopal Church. The lady said: "I was staying in Virginia, some hundred miles away from home, when one morning about eleven o'clock, I felt an overpowering sleepiness, which drowsiness was quite unusual, and which caused me to lie down. In my sleep I saw quite distinctly my home in Richmond in flames. The fire had broken out in one wing of the house, which I saw with dismay was where I kept all my best dresses. The people were all trying to check the flames, but it was no use. My husband was there, walking about before the burning house, carrying a portrait in his hand. Everything was quite clear and distinct, exactly as if I had actually been present and seen everything. After a time I woke up, and going downstairs told my friends the strange dream I had had. They laughed at me, and made such game of my vision that I did my best to think no more about it. I was traveling about, a day or two passed, and when Sunday came I found myself in a church where some relatives were worshipping. When I entered the pew they looked rather strange, and as soon as the service was over I asked them what was the matter. 'Don't be alarmed,' they said 'there is nothing serious.' Then they handed me a postcard from my husband which simply said, 'House burned out; covered by insurance.' **The day was the date upon which my dream occurred.** I hastened home, and then I learned that everything had happened exactly as I had seen it. The fire had broken out in the wing I had seen blazing. My clothes were all burnt, and the oddest thing about it was that my husband, having rescued a favorite picture from the burning building, had carried it about among the crowd for some time before he could find a place in which to put it safely."

A well-authenticated case is that of the wreck of the ship "Strathmore." Stead relates the story as follows: "The father of a son who had sailed in the 'Strathmore,' an emigrant ship outbound from Clyde, saw one night the ship foundering amid the waves, and saw that his son, with some others had escaped safely to a desert island near which the wreck had taken place. He was so much impressed by this vision that he wrote to the owner of the 'Strathmore,' telling him what he had seen. His information

57

was scouted; but after a while the 'Strathmore' became overdue, and the owner became uneasy. Day followed day, and still no tidings of the missing ship. Then, like Pharaoh's butler, the owner remembered his sins one day, and hunted up the letter describing the vision. It supplied at least a theory to account for the vessel's disappearance. All outward-bound ships were requested to look out for any survivors on the island indicated in the vision. These orders being obeyed, the survivors of the 'Strathmore' were found exactly where the father had seen them."

Another interesting case is reported by the Society previously mentioned. It reports that Dr. Golinski, a physician of Kremeutchug, Russia, was taking an after-dinner nap in the afternoon, about half-past three o'clock. He had a vision in which he saw himself called out on a professional visit, which took him to a little room with dark hangings. To the right of the door he saw a chest of drawers, upon which rested a little paraffin lamp of special pattern, different from anything he had ever seen before. On the left of the door, he saw a woman suffering from . a severe hemorrhage. He then saw himself giving her professional treatment. Then he awoke, suddenly, and saw that it was just half-past four o'clock. Then comes, the strange sequel. Within ten minutes after he awoke, he was called out on a professional visit, and on entering the bedroom he saw all the details that had appeared to him in his vision. There was the chest of drawers — there was the peculiar lamp — there was the woman on the bed suffering from the hemorrhage. Upon inquiry he found that she had grown worse between three and four o'clock, and had anxiously desired that he come to her about that time, finally dispatching a messenger for him at half-past four, the moment at which he awoke.

We could fill page after page with these interesting and well-authenticated instances, but our lack of space prevents. We have stated enough to illustrate the principle, and then, besides, many of our readers will know of many similar instances in the actual experience of themselves, relatives or friends. Volumes would not contain all the true stories of phenomena of this kind — and still people smile in a superior way at the mere suggestion of the phenomena.

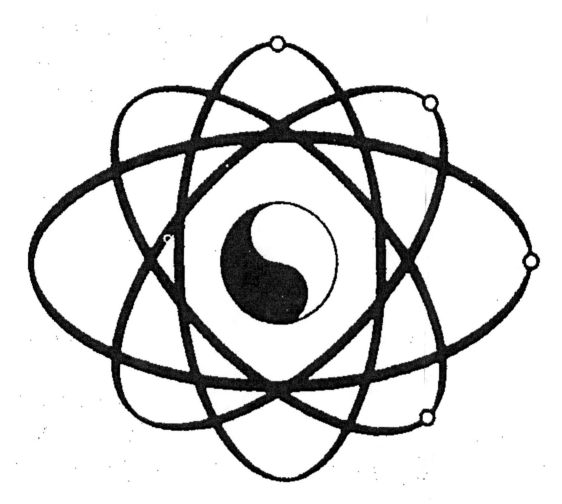

Lesson IX.
Past Time Psychomancy

AS WE have previously stated, "Time Psychomancy" is a term used to designate that phase of the phenomena in which one senses objects, events, persons, etc., in the records of the past; and also in which he senses the indications of the future—"the shadows of coming events."

For convenience, we shall separate our consideration of the subject into two parts, viz.:

(1) Fast Time Psychomancy; and

(2) Future Time Psychomancy.

Fast Time Psychomancy is that phase of the phenomena which enables one to use his Astral Vision to explore the records of the past, arid we shall now proceed to examine.

61

The first question that naturally arises in the minds of careful students, in connection with this phase of the phenomena, is, "How is the person able to sense the scenes, occurrences, and objects of the past? There are no vibrations emanating from past scenes, and as they no longer exist, how can anyone see them, by Astral Vision, or by any other means?" This question is a most proper one, for even those who readily grasp the explanation of Space Psychomancy find themselves at a loss to understand the Past Time Phenomena without a knowledge of the Occult Teachings on the subjects.

THE AKASHIC RECORDS

The secret of Past Time Psychomancy is found in the Occult Teachings of the "Akashic Records." by which is meant that on the higher planes of Universal Substance, there are to be found records of all that has happened and occurred during the entire World Cycle of which the present time forms a part. These records are preserved until the termination of the World Cycle, when they pass away with the World of which they are a record. This does not mean that there is any Great Book in which the doings, good and bad, of people are written down by the Recording Angel, as popular fanciful legends has it. But it does mean that there is a scientific occult basis for the popular legend, in spite of the sneers of the skeptics. We must turn to modern science for a corroboration. It is now taught by scientists that there is no such thing as a destruction of Energy, but that Energy always exists in some form. The Occult Teachings verify this, and go further, when they state that every action, thought, happening, event, occurrence, etc., no matter how small or insignificant, leaves an indelible record on the Akasha (or Universal Ether) with which Space is filled. In other words, every action, or scene, that

62

has ever occurred or existed in the past, has left an impression in the Universal Ether, or Akasha, where it may be read by developed Psychomancy.

There is nothing especially wonderful about this, when you compare it with other facts in nature. Astronomy teaches us that light travels at the rate of 186,000 miles a second—and that there are fixed stars in space so far removed from the Earth that theft light leaving them hundreds, yes, thousands, of years ago, is only now reaching our sight. In other words, when we look at some of the fixed stars, we do not see them as they now are, or where they now are, but merely see them where and how they were hundreds of years ago when the rays of light left them. Astronomers tell us that if one of these stars happened to be blotted out of existence hundreds of years ago, we would be still seeing the light that left them before the event—in other words would be seeing them hundreds of years after they had ceased to be. And our children, and children's children, for several generations would still see them, and would not learn of the terrible catastrophe for hundreds of years after it actually happened. The vibrations of light once set into motion would persist for centuries, and even for thousands of years after their source had disappeared. This is no wild occult fancy, but a well-proven and thoroughly-established scientific fact, as any one may see for himself by reference to any work on astronomy. And the same is true of waves of electricity, or electronic emanations, or waves of any kind of energy. Really, even in the physical view of things, nothing can exist without leaving a record in the Universal Ether. And so the Occult Teachings now find their corroboration in Modern Science.

Another illustration is found in the phenomena of the Memory of Man. Stored away in our brain cells are records of things, events, scenes, occurrences, people, and objects, registered there in past years. You often find yourself thinking

63

about people, things and events of years long since passed away—and by a mere effort of the will you bring the records of these people, things, or events before your mental vision and see them reproduced in detail. Dissect a brain-cell and you will find no trace of the thing there—but nevertheless every exercise of memory proves that the record is there. And there is nothing more wonderful, or miraculous, in the Akashic Records of Past Events, than there is in the Memory Record of Past Events! The Universal Ether, or Akasha, has within itself a true and full record of anything, and everything, that has ever existed within its space. And if one develops the power to read these records at will, he has a full and complete key to the past, from the speaking of the Creative Word which began this great World Cycle.

But, in order to avoid a misapprehension, we must say to our students that none but the most advanced and highly-developed Occultists and Masters have clear access to the planes upon Which these records are to be found. The majority of Psychomancers merely see on the "Lower Astral Plane" a reflection of the Akashic Records, which reflection may be compared to the reflection of the trees and landscape in a pond of water, which of course, is often more or Jess imperfect—distorted and disturbed by the ripples and waves occasioned by the passing breezes,. and sometimes being made muddy and clouded. The records of the Past, open to the average Psychomancer, are merely **"reflections of records,"** which are apt to be more or less distorted, Or cloudy, by reason of the disturbances of the surface' of the reflecting medium. This is a brief and simple statement of an important Occult scientific truth, which would require volumes to explain technically. The illustration of the reflecting surface of the water, however, is so true to the real facts that the student may confidently adopt the same as his mental image of the phenomena of Past Time Psychomancy.

In actual practice we find the phenomena **of** Past Time Psychomancy manifested principally along the line of Psychometry and Crystal Gazing, the consideration of which phases of phenomena has been made in previous lessons in this book. There ate to be found, however, many instances of at least a partial manifestation of this phase of power among individuals in everyday life, who when meeting a person frequently get impressions (more or less correct) of his or her past life, past scenes, etc.

The German writer, Zschokke, in his autobiography, writes as follows regarding this power of Past Time Psychomancy possessed by him, and which was often set into operation when he came into the presence of strangers for the first time. He states: "It has happened to me sometimes, on my first meeting with strangers, as I silently listened to their discourse, that their former life, with many trifling circumstances therewith connected, or frequently some particular scene in that life, has passed quite involuntarily, and, as it were, dream-like, yet perfectly distinct, before me. During this time I usually feel so entirely absorbed in the contemplation of the stranger's life, that at last I no longer see clearly the face of the unknown wherein I undesignedly read, nor distinctly hear the voices of the speakers, which before served in some measure as a commentary on the text of their features. For a long time I held such visions as delusions of the fancy, and the more so as they showed me even the dress and emotions of the actors, rooms, furniture, and other accessories, but I soon discovered otherwise.

"On one occasion, in a gay mood, I narrated to my family the secret history of a seamstress who had just before quitted the room. I had never seen the young woman before. Nevertheless, the hearers were astonished and laughed, and would not be persuaded but that I had a previous acquaintance with her and the facts of her former life, inasmuch as what I had stated was perfectly true. I was not the less astonished than they to find that my vision agreed with reality."

"I then gave more attention to the subject, and as often as propriety allowed of it, I related to those whose lives had passed before me, the substance of my visions, in order to obtain from them a contradiction or verification thereof. On every occasion the confirmation followed, not without amazement on the part of those who gave it."

"One day, in the city of Waldshut, I entered an inn (the Vine) in company with two young students. We supped with a numerous company at the table d'hote, where the guests were making very merry with the peculiarities of the Swiss, with Mesmer's magnetism, Lavater's physiognomy, etc. One of my companions, whose national pride was wounded by their mockery, begged me to make some reply, particularly to a handsome young man who, sat opposite to us. and who had allowed himself extraordinary license. This man's life was .at that moment presented to my mind. I turned to him, and asked whether he would answer me candidly if I related to him some of the most secret passages of his life, I knowing as little of him personally as he did of me. He promised, if I were correct, to admit it frankly. I then related what my vision had shown me, and the whole company were made acquainted with the private history of the young merchant—his school years, his youthful errors, and, lastly, with a fault committed in reference to the strong-box of his principal. I described the uninhabited room with whitened walls, where, to the right of the brown door, on a table, stood a black money-box, etc; A dead silence prevailed during the whole narrative, which I alone occasionally interrupted by inquiring whether I spoke the truth. The startled young man confirmed every particular, and even, what I had scarcely expected, the last mentioned. Touched by his candor, I shook hands with him, and said no more. He is, probably, still living."

Lesson X.
Future Time Psychomancy

F UTURE Time Psychomancy," as the term itself indicates, is the name given to that class of phenomena in which one is able to sense the Astral Plane impression of coming events—the psychic shadows thrown before by coming events. In order to give the student a technical nature of the occult cause behind this phenomena would require volumes of the deepest metaphysical lore, which field is foreign to the purposes of this work which deals with phenomena alone, and does not enter into the metaphysical side of the subject.

It will be sufficient for the student to understand that in the Astral as well as on the Physical Plane, "**Coming Events cast their Shadows Before**." Without entering into a discussion of Destiny or Fate, or anything of that kind, it may be stated that **when Causes are set into motion, the Effects follow,** unless other Causes intervene. In some cases certain effects have been averted by reason of the previous Vision— in such cases **the other Causes intervened**, which showed that the matter was not wholly "cut and dried." It is like a man walking toward a precipice—he will walk over unless he is warned in some way. He is not "fated" to walk over but over he will go, unless warned and prevented. Do you see what we mean?

On the other hand, there seem to be cases in which the person seems unable to escape the Effect of Causes once set into motion— he even Seems to run into the effect, while seeking to escape it. In this connection the little fable of the Persians may be quoted. The story goes that a friend was with Solomon when the Angel of Death entered and gazed at him fixedly. Upon learning who the strange visitor was, the friend said to Solomon, "Pray transport me on thy magic carpet to Damascus, that I may escape this dread messenger." And Solomon complied with his request, and the man was instantly magically transported to Damascus. Then said the Angel of Death to Solomon: "O Solomon, the reason that I gazed so intently at thy friend was because I had orders from On High to take him from the body at Damascus, and lo! finding him here at Jerusalem, I was sore perplexed as to how to obey my orders. But, thou, by transporting him to Damascus hath rendered my task an easy one. Many thanks, for thy help at thy friend's suggestion, O King!" And saying which the Angel of Death was wafted away to Damascus to take the man, according to orders.

The phenomena of Premonitions, Prevision, and Second Sight, are all forms or phases of Future Time Psychomancy. In these various forms the phenomena is of quite common and frequent occurrence, and is met with all over the world. In the Isle of Skye many persons possess the gift of Second Sight in varying degree, but they claim that a native of the island loses the power when he moves to the mainland. In the same way the Scotch Highlander (among whose people the gift is quite common) is said to sometimes lose the faculty when he removes to the lowlands. The Westphalian peasants also are noted for the power of Second Sight.

An instance of this phase of the phenomena, well known in England, is that connected with the assassination of Mr. Percival in the lobby of the House of Commons. This deed was foreseen by John Williams, a Cornish mine manager, some nine days before its actual occurrence, the vision being perfect down to the most minute details. Williams had the vision three times in succession. He saw a small man, dressed in a blue coat and white waistcoat, enter the lobby of the House of Commons, when another person, dressed in a snuff-colored coat, stepped forward and drawing a pistol from an inside pocket fired at and shot the little man, the bullet lodging in the left breast. He seemed to ask some bystander who was the victim, and he received the reply that it was Mr. Percival, the Chancellor of the Exchequer. Williams was so much wrought up over the vision, that he seriously contemplated going to London to warn the victim, but his friends, to whom he told the story, ridiculed him and persuaded him not to go on "a fool's errand." A few days later the news was received of the assassination of Mr. Percival, in precisely the manner indicated by the vision.

George Fox the Quaker, experienced the impression of "a waft of death" about Cromwell when he met him riding at Hampton Court, shortly before his fatal illness. Fox also foretold the expulsion of the "Rump Parliament;" the restoration of Charles II; and the Fire of London. Caesar's wife had a warning of her husband's death. The Bible is filled with similar instances.

We will conclude this lesson with a recital of the wonderful instance of Cazotte, whose prediction, and its literal fulfillment, are now matters of French history. La Harpe tells the story as follows:

"It appears but as yesterday, and yet, nevertheless, it was at the beginning of the year 1788. We were dining with one of our brethren at the Academy—a man of considerable wealth and genius. The conversation became serious; much admiration was expressed on the revolution in thought which Voltaire had effected, and it was agreed that it was his first claim to the reputation he enjoyed. We concluded that the revolution must soon be consummated; that it was indispensable that superstition and fanaticism should give place to philosophy, and we began to calculate the probability of the period when this should be, and which of the present company should live to see it. The oldest complained that they could scarcely flatter themselves with the hope; the younger rejoiced that they might entertain this very probable expectation; and they congratulated the Academy especially for having . prepared this great work, and for having been the great rallying point, the centre, and the prime mover of the liberty of thought.

"One only of the guests had not taken part in all the joyousness of this conversation, and had even gently and cheerfully checked our splendid enthusiasm. This was Cazotte, an amiable and original man, but unhappily infatuated with the reveries of the illuminati. He spoke, and with the most serious tone.. 'Gentlemen,' said he, 'be satisfied; you will all see this great and sublime revolution, which you so much desire. You know that I am a little inclined to prophesy; I repeat, you will see it.' He was answered by the common rejoinder: 'One need not be a conjuror to see that.' 'Be it so; but perhaps one must be a little more than conjuror for what remains for me to tell you. Do you know what will be the consequence of this revolution—what will be the consequence to all of you, and what will be the immediate result — the well-established effect — the thoroughly recognized consequence to all of you who are here present?' 'Ah!' said Condorcet, with his insolent and half-suppressed smile, 'let us hear — a philosopher is not sorry to encounter a prophet.' 'You,

Monsieur de Condorcet—you will yield up your last breath on the floor of a dungeon; you will die from poison, which you will have taken, in order to escape from execution—from poison which the happiness of that time will oblige you to carry about your person.'

"'Monsieur de Chamfort, you will open your veins with twenty-two cuts of a razor, and yet you will not die until some months afterward.' They looked at each other, and laughed again. 'You, Monsieur Vicq d'Azir, you will not open your own veins, but you will cause yourself to be bled six times in one day, during a parozysm of the gout, in order to make more sure of your end, and you will die in the night. You, Monsieur de Nicolai, you will die upon the scaffold; you, Monsieur Bailly, on the scaffold; you, Monsieur de Malesherbes, on the scaffold.' 'Ah! God be thanked,' exclaimed Roucher, 'and what of I?' 'You! you also will die upon the scaffold.' 'Yes,' replied Chamfort, 'but when will all this happen?' 'Six years will not pass over, before all that I have said to you shall be accomplished.'

"'Here are some astonishing miracles (and, this time, it was I myself (La Harpe) who spoke), but you have not included me in your list.' 'But you will be there, as an equally extraordinary miracle; you will then be a Christian.' Vehement exclamations on all sides. 'Ah,' replied Chamfort, 'I am comforted; if we shall perish only when La Harpe shall be a Christian, we are immortal.'

"'As for that,' then observed Madame la Duchesse de Grammont, 'we women, we are happy to be counted for nothing in these revolutions; when I say for nothing, it is not that we do not always mix ourselves up with them a little; but it is a received maxim that they take no notice of us, and of our sex.' 'Your sex, ladies, will not protect you this time; and you had far better meddle with nothing, for you will be treated entirely as men, without any difference what ever.' 'But what, then, are you really telling us of, Monsieur Cazotte? You are preaching to us the end of the world.' 'I know nothing on this subject; but what I do know is, that you; Madame la Duchesse, will be conducted to the scaffold, you and many other ladies with you, in the cart of the executioner, and with your hands tied behind your backs.' 'Ah! I hope that, in that case, I shall at least have a carriage hung in black.' 'No, Madame; higher ladies than yourself will go, like you, in the common car, with their hands tied behind them.' 'Higher ladies! what! the princesses of the blood?' 'Still more exalted personages.' Here a sensible emotion pervaded the whole company, and the countenance of the host was dark and lowering; they began to feel that the joke was become too serious.

"Madame de Grammont, in order to dissipate the cloud, took no notice of the reply, and contented herself with saying in a careless tone:

'You see that he will not leave me even a confessor!' 'No, Madame, you will not have one— neither you, nor any one besides. The last victim to whom this favor will be afforded will be——' He stopped for a moment. 'Well! who then will be the happy mortal to whom this prerogative will be given?' ''Tis the only one which he will have then retained—and that will be the king of France. '

The amazing sequel to this historical prediction is that **it was verified in every detail**, as all students of the French Revolution know—**and all within the six years,** as Cazotte foretold.

Lesson XI.
Dream Psychomancy

THE Student will have noted that in many cases mentioned in these lessons, the Psychomantic vision manifested during physical sleep. The reason of this occurrence is that in the majority of persons the physical nature, when awake, holds the attention of the individual to such an extent as to prevent him from manifesting the psychic faculties clearly. But when the physical body sinks into sleep then the field is clear for the exercise of the Astral Senses, which not being fatigued, are in fine condition to manifest. In fact the majority of persons do manifest Psychomancy during sleep, but have little or no recollection of the same when waking, beyond indistinct recollections of "dreams," etc. Still, many of you who read these lines will have a more or less clear remembrance of certain "dreams" in which you seemed to visit other places, scenes, lands, countries, etc., seeing strange faces, landscapes, etc., and upon awakening were somewhat annoyed at having been brought back from your pleasant travels.

It is not our intention to enter into an extended consideration of the general subject of Dreams, at this time and place. We write these few lines merely for the purpose of calling your attention to the fact that the phenomena of Psychomancy very frequently manifests itself in dreams, for the reasons stated above. The principle in both the waking and dream phenomena is precisely the same, the apparent difference being that the dreamer very seldom carries back with him a clear and connected memory of his vision, while the waking person is able to impress his Astral vision upon a wide-awake physical brain, there to be remembered.

You will find several instances of Dream Psychomancy recorded in the various lessons of this work, inserted for the purpose of illustrating the several phases of the phenomena. In such cases we have made no distinction between the Psychomantic phenomena experienced in dreams on the one hand, and that experienced in the waking state on the other hand. The principle is the same in both cases, and there is no necessity for making any such distinction between the phenomena occurring under any of the several general classes. But as we still have to spare a few pages of the space allotted to us in the preparation of these lessons, we think that we should give you a few more of the many interesting cases .of record.

A well-known and interesting ease is that mentioned in the Proceedings of the Psychical Research Society, of London. It is related as follows:

On September 9th, 1848, at the siege of Mooltan, Major General R. was most severely and dangerously wounded; and, supposing himself to be dying, asked one of the officers with him to take the ring off his finger and send it to his wife, who at the time was fully 150 miles distant at Ferozepore.

"On the night of September 9th, 1848," writes his wife, "I was lying on my bed, between sleeping and waking, when I distinctly saw my husband being carried off the field seriously wounded, and heard his voice, saying, 'Take this ring off my finger and send it to my wife.' All the next day I could not get the sight or the voice out of my mind. In due time I heard of General R. having been seriously wounded in the assault of Mooltan. He survived, however, and is still living. It was not for some time after the siege that I heard from General L., the officer who helped to carry my husband off the field, that the request as to the ring was actually made by him, just as I heard it at Ferozepore at that very time."

The following, related by Mrs. Crowe, is interesting, particularly in its aspect as a warning:

"A few years ago, Dr. Watson, now residing at Glasgow, dreamt that he received a summons to attend a patient at a place some miles from where he was living; that he started on horseback, and that as he was crossing a moor, he saw a bull making furiously at him, whose horns he escaped only by taking refuge on a spot inaccessible to the animal, where he waited a long time till some people, observing his situation, came to his assistance and released him. While at breakfast the following morning the summons came, and smiling at the odd co-incidence (as he thought it), he started on horseback. He was quite ignorant of the road he had to go, but by and by he arrived at the moor, which he recognized, and presently the bull appeared, coming full tilt towards him. But his dream had shown him the place of refuge, for which he instantly made, and there he spent three or four hours besieged by the animal, till the country people set him free. Dr. Watson declared that but for the dream he should not have known in what direction to run for safety."

This case is an instance of Future Time Psychomancy, as the student will readily see. Here is another case coming under the same classification. It is related by Dr. Lee:

Mrs. Hannah Green, the housekeeper of a country family in

Oxfordshire, dreamt one night that she had been left alone in the house on a Sunday evening, and that hearing a knock at the door of the chief entrance, she went to it and found confronting her an ugly tramp, armed with a big club, who forced himself into the house in spite of her struggles, striking her insensible with his club during the conflict. She awoke at this point. A considerable period of time elapsed, and she had almost forgotten her dream until it was recalled in a startling manner. She was then in charge of an isolated mansion at Kensington, and on a Sunday afternoon, when the servants had taken a holiday, leaving her alone, she was startled by a loud knock at the door. At once the memory of her dream flashed before her with singular vividness and remarkable force. She knew that she was alone, but for the purpose of frightening away the intruder she lighted a lamp on the hail table, and afterward in other places in the house, and also rang the bells violently in different parts of the house. She also made sure that the doors and windows were fastened. She succeeded in scaring off the man, by making him believe that the house was occupied by the family, or several people at least, but not until she had thrown up the window over the stair landing, and there to her intense terror saw the identical man of her dream, armed with the same club, and demanding an entrance. Had she not been warned by the dream of several years previous, she would have met with a fate such as she had dreamed of.

The following case of Dream Psychomancy, which is a good example of Astral Projection during sleep, is related by a correspondent of the Psychical Research Society, as follows:

"One morning in December, 1836, he had the following dream, or, he would prefer to call it, revelation. He found himself suddenly at the gate of Major N. M.'s avenue, many miles from his home. Close to him was a group of persons, one of whom was a woman with a basket on her arm, the rest men, four of whom were tenants of his own, while the others were unknown to him. Some of the strangers seemed to be assaulting H. W., one of his tenants, and he interfered. 'I struck violently at the man on my left, and then with greater violence at the man's face on my right.. Finding, to my surprise, that I had not knocked down either, I struck again and again with all the violence of a man frenzied at the sight of my poor friend's murder. To my great amazement I saw my arms, although visible to my eye, were without substance, and the bodies of the men I struck at and my own came close together after each blow through the shadowy arms I struck with. My blows were delivered with more extreme violence than I ever think I exerted, but I became painfully convinced of my incompetency. I have no consciousness of what happened after this feeling of unsubstantiality came upon me.' Next morning A. experienced the stiffness and soreness of violent bodily exercise, and was informed by his wife that in the course of the night he had much alarmed her by striking out again and again with his arms in a terrific manner, 'as if fighting for his life.' He, in turn, informed her of his dream, and begged her to remember the names of those actors in it who were known to him. On the morning of the following day (Wednesday) A. received a letter from his agent, who resided in the town close to the scene of the dream, informing that his tenant had been found on Tuesday morning at Major N. M.'s gate, speechless and apparently dying from a fracture of the skull, and that there was no trace of the murderers. That night A. started for the town, and arrived there on Thursday morning. On his way to **a** meeting of magistrates he met the senior magistrate of that part of the country, and requested him to give orders for the arrest of the three men whom, besides H. W., he had recognized in his dream, and to have them examined separately. This was at once done. The three men gave identical accounts of the occurrence, and all named the woman who was with them. She was then arrested, and gave precisely similar testimony. They said. that between eleven and twelve on the Monday night they had been walking homewards altogether along the road, when they were overtaken by three strangers, two of whom savagely assaulted H.W,, while the other prevented his friends from interfering. H. W. did not die, but was never the same man afterwards; he subsequently emigrated."

Stead relates the following case, which was imparted to him as a truthful and correct account of the vision of a murder seen in all of its details by a brother of the murdered man. It is a case of Astral Projection, undoubtedly:

"St. Eglos is situated about ten miles from the Atlantic, and not quite so far from the old market town of Trebodwina. Hart and George Northey were brothers, and from childhood their lives had been marked by the strongest brotherly affection. Hart and George Northey had never been separated from their birth until George became a sailor, Hart meantime joining his father in business. On the 8th of February, 1840, while George Northey's ship was lying in port at St. Helena, he had the following strange dream:

"'Last night I dreamt my brother was at Trebodwina Market, and that I was with him, quite close by his side, during the whole of the market transactions. Although I could see and hear everything which passed around me, I felt sure that it was not my bodily presence which thus accompanied him, but my shadow, or rather my spiritual presence, for he seemed quite Unconscious that I was near him. I felt that my being thus present in this strange way betokened some hidden danger which he was destined to meet, and which I knew my presence could not avert, for I could not speak to warn him of his peril.'

The brother having collected considerable money then started on his ride homeward. The story then continues:

"'My terror gradually increased as Hart approached the hamlet of Polkerrow, until I was in a perfect frenzy, frantically desirous, yet unable, to warn my brother in some way and prevent him going further. I suddenly became aware of two dark shadows thrown across the road. I felt my brother's hour had come, and I was powerless to aid him! Two men appeared, whom I instantly recognized as notorious poachers, who lived in a lonely wood near St. Eglos. The men wished him "Good-night," maister," civilly enough. He replied, and entered into conversation with them about some work he had promised them. After a few minutes they asked him for some money. The elder of the two brothers, who was standing near the horse's head, said, "Mr. Northey, we know you have just come from Trebodwina market with plenty of money in your pockets; we are desperate men, and you bean't going to leave this place until we've got that money, so hand over." My brother made no reply, except to slash at him with the whip and spur the horse at him.

'"The younger of the ruffians instantly drew a pistol and fired. Hart dropped lifeless from the saddle, and one of the villains held him by the throat with a grip of iron for some minutes, as though to make assurance doubly sure, and crush out any particle of life my poor brother might have left. The murderers secured the horse to a tree in the orchard, and, having rifled the corpse, they dragged it up the stream, concealing it under the overhanging banks of the water-course. They then carefully covered over all marks of blood on the road, and hid the pistol in the thatch of a disused hut close to the roadside.; then, setting the horse free to gallop home alone, they decamped across the country to their own cottage.'

"The vessel left St. Helena next day, and reached Plymouth in due course. George Northey had during the whole of the voyage home, never altered his conviction that Hart had been killed as he had dreamt, and that retribution was by his means to fall on the murderers."

The sequel shows that the murder was actually committed in precisely the manner in which it had appeared to the brother in the dream. The crime aroused universal horror and indignation, and every effort was made to discover the murderers and bring them to justice. Two brothers named Hightwood were suspected, and a search of their cottage revealed bloodstained garments, but no trace of the pistol was to be found, although the younger brother admitted having had one and lost it. The story continues:

"Both brothers were arrested and brought before the magistrates. The evidence against them was certainly not strong, but their manner seemed that of guilty men. They were ordered to take their trial at the forthcoming assizes at Trebodwina. They each confessed in the hope of saving their lives, and both were sentenced to be hanged. There was, however, some doubt about the pistol. Before the execution George Northey arrived from St. Helena, and declared that the pistol was in the thatch of the old cottage close by the place where they murdered Hart Northey, and where they hid it. 'How did you know?' he was asked. George Northey replied: 'I saw the foul deed committed in a dream I had the night of the murder, when at St. Helena.' A pistol was found, as George Northey had predicted, in the thatch of the ruined cottage."

We trust that we have established the identity of Waking Psychomancy, and Dream Psychomancy, to your satisfaction.

Finis.

COUNT SAINT GERMAIN IN LAB
A Psychic impression by Carol Ann Rodriguez

DragonStar book series continued...

HOW TO TRAVEL TO OTHER DIMENSIONS

AN 11-LESSON COURSE ON WHAT YOU WILL FIND WHEN YOU GET THERE

☐ Written with the assistance of S. Panchadasi, this course by DragonStar paves the way for the student to enter other dimensions and travel freely on the various layers that have been identified by mystics for centuries as the seven planes of the astral world.

"Time travel to the past and future is possible as we soar from place to place, from region to region," says DragonStar. Long thought to be a dangerous journey, here is the means by which all can accomplish this mode of spiritual travel without having to stress about negative entities blocking one's path to higher awareness. Find out where these other dimensions are located. How one can visit these dimensions. Identifying the good entities from the bad ones. Discovering the resting place of all souls. Learning the law of the astral and how it can manifest. How to change vibrations at will. Exploring the many wonderful sights to be found. How to become one with the light. Here are some of the oldest teachings known to the masters of the esoteric brought up to date and taught in a concise manner. ONLY $12.00.

DEVELOP YOUR LATENT PARANORMAL POWERS

☐ Much has been written on developing one's latent psychic abilities. This book goes well beyond the gift of ESP. Come along with the master DragonStar and William Walker Atkinson as they explore the fascinating world of the "supernatural" phenomena. Now you can pick up a crystal ball and see the future. Know how to use a Magick Mirror. See through slid objects. "Feel" the thoughts of others. Learn to "read" minds. Tell the past association of any object. Dematerialize one's self. Journey through time and space. Travel in the past and future. Know your own destiny and fate. Unlock the phenomenon of psychic dreams and visions. Take part in distant scenes, events and conversations. Tune into the Akashic Records. YES! It's only 112 pages, but BIG THINGS do come in small packages. Be uplifted. Be entertained. And above all else...become aware! ONLY $12.00.

CANDLE MAGICK DIVINATION: GOOD LUCK, GOOD FORTUNE

Secrets of Your Future...Revealed in the Flame

☐ Candle burning has for centuries been a popular form of divination. Now YOU can learn to mark a candle for spiritual use. Learn about the special preparations needed when using incense and oil. Selecting the right candles and preparing them for ritualistic use. Watching the wax. Locating lost objects. Shapes to be found in wax and smoke and what they mean for YOUR future.

One little known aspect of candle burning is the ability to channel ones psychic energies in order to see the future. Whether you use candles, crystals, pendulum, ink, lead, dice, the flights of birds or anything else...what you are really doing is opening your end of a channel to higher wisdom. This is a practical spell book that will work for you for years to come. Dozens of different methods of divination are given, explained, and the means by which they can be utilized in your everyday life. A real Third Eye opener! ONLY $12.00